Better Homes and Gardens®

HOMEMADE

BREAD

COOK BOOK

Sample these delicious *Cinnamon Crescents* just once, and you'll discover that they're perfect for any occasion. The icing-topped coffee cakes are filled with a spicy raisin-nut mixture. The recipe is on page 36.

On the cover: You'll be more than pleased to serve any one of these tasty yeast breads—frosted *Cinnamon Rolls,* poppy seed-topped *Batter Rolls,* and hearty loaves of *Whole Wheat Bread.* See index for page numbers.

BETTER HOMES AND GARDENS® BOOKS

Editorial Director: Don Dooley
Managing Editor: Malcolm E. Robinson   Art Director: John Berg
Asst. Managing Editor: Lawrence D. Clayton   Asst. Art Director: Randall Yontz
Food Editor: Nancy Morton
Senior Food Editor: Joyce Trollope
Associate Editors: Sharyl Heiken, Rosemary C. Hutchinson
Assistant Editors: Elizabeth Strait, Sandra Mapes,
Catherine Penney, Elizabeth Walter
Designers: Harijs Priekulis, Faith Berven

CONTENTS

Our seal assures you that every recipe in *Homemade Bread Cook Book* is endorsed by the Better Homes and Gardens Test Kitchen. Each recipe is tested for family appeal, practicality, and deliciousness.

Time-Worthy Baking

Why spend hours of your time making homemade bread? After all, you can go to your supermarket, grab some bread or a coffee cake off the shelf, and have something ready in 20 minutes.

Actually, there are several reasons why many homemakers make their own bread. Like generations of homemakers before them, some view this cooking skill as a means of self-expression. Others cite the satisfaction they feel when family or friends say, "That bread's great." Still others prefer the homemade because it is homemade and it tastes so good.

Regardless of your reason for wanting to make homemade bread, the *Homemade Bread Cook Book* is just right for you. You say you've never baked bread before? Don't let that deter you. You will find simple-to-follow directions for all of the recipes in this book. And for those of you who have mastered the bread-baking skills, there are new and intriguing recipes for you, too.

Today, homemade bread is easier to make than ever before. "Why," you ask? Because preparation methods have been refined by yeast and flour manufacturers who are continually developing techniques for simplifying bread preparation. One of these recent techniques is a mixing method that is referred to in this book as the 'easy-mix method.' Many of the yeast-bread recipes are prepared using this method.

If you prefer the conventional method of preparing yeast breads (dissolving yeast in water), there are recipes in this book for you, too.

Whether you use the easy-mix method or the conventional method when baking bread, you will get equally good nutritional results. Remember that bread plays an important role in the diet. Together with cereal products, bread is one of the Basic Four Food Groups. Four servings of foods from this group should be eaten daily, together with foods from the other three food groups.

When baking bread, always use enriched all-purpose flour because it has iron and the B vitamins, thiamine, riboflavin, and niacin added, all of which figure in good nutrition.

As an aid to you in your bread-baking endeavors, pictures and tip boxes showing you 'how-to' prepare or shape breads and coffee cakes have been included throughout the book. From the beginning of the book to the end, you will find a wide selection of taste-tempting recipes from which to choose.

So, page through the *Homemade Bread Cook Book* and pick out some recipes that appeal to you. Whether you bake a yeast or a quick bread, your efforts will be appreciated by all who enjoy eating freshly baked breads.

New-fashioned variety of breads

← For a mid-morning treat, serve milk with one of these—*Cheesecake Bread Ring, Cinnamonjam Squares, Toasted Coconut Coffee Cake,* or *Fig-Oatmeal Muffins.* (See index for page numbers.)

ENTICING YEAST BREADS

Nothing whets the appetite like the aroma of a yeast bread baking in the oven. So, why not treat your family and guests to these aromatic, delicious-tasting products.

At the beginning of this section of the book, you will find information about ingredients and some preparation pointers, especially pertinent to yeast breads, that will aid you in your baking. In addition, basic bread and roll recipes, made by both the easy-mix and conventional methods, are handy for your ready reference on pages 12 and 14.

As you look over the delicious-sounding bread, roll, coffee cake, and sweet roll recipes, you are sure to find many that you'll want to try. Add these enticing yeast-bread recipes to your own list of favorites.

Choose from this array of breads. Included are *Whole Wheat Rolls, French Chocolate Coffee Cake, Bacon Bread,* and *Cornmeal Loaves.* (See index for page numbers.)

Yeast-Bread Tips

Before you begin your baking adventures with yeast breads, it will be helpful to know something about the ingredients that are used, plus a few preparation techniques. So, whether you're a beginning bread baker or an old-hand at it, take note of this information.

INGREDIENTS

Flour is the major ingredient in breads. The gluten in wheat flour forms the framework that gives bread its structure. The most common type of flour used in baking is all-purpose flour, made from a blend of soft- and hard-wheat varieties. For good nutrition, be sure that the flour you buy is enriched.

When baking bread, it is not necessary to sift the *all-purpose flour* before it is measured. However, if you don't plan to sift the flour, the best and most accurate way to measure it is to stir the flour in the canister, spoon it lightly into the measuring cup, and level off the cup with the straight edge of a spatula or knife. Do not tap or shake the cup to pack down the flour before measuring, or you will get an excess amount of flour.

Unbleached white flour can be substituted for all-purpose flour in the bread recipes in this book. However, be sure that you buy enriched unbleached flour for added nutrition.

Specialty flours, such as whole wheat, rye, brown rice, and barley, add interesting textures and flavors to breads. You should combine most of these flours with all-purpose flour, as they do not have enough gluten on their own to effect proper bread structure. Also, you should measure these flours by first stirring the flour, then by lightly spooning it into a measuring cup and leveling off.

Yeast is the leavening in bread. Actually, yeast is a living plant that grows in warm, moist doughs. It gives off bubbles of gas, thereby causing the dough to rise.

Active dry yeast, the type called for in the recipes in this book, is available in packages containing about 1 tablespoon of yeast. It is especially simple to use in recipes made by the easy-mix method. For this method, you mix the dry yeast with part of the flour, add the warm liquid ingredients, and beat with an electric mixer. The mixer saves much hand-beating.

Compressed yeast is also available and can be used in recipes that call for softening the yeast in water (conventional method). Substitute one 0.6-ounce cake of compressed yeast for each package of active dry yeast.

For those recipes made by the conventional method, soften the compressed yeast in *lukewarm* water (85°) and the active dry yeast in *warm* water (110°). A word of caution—be sure that liquids used to dissolve the yeast or liquids added to yeast mixtures are not too hot. Adhere to the temperatures given in the recipes. The first few times you bake bread, check the temperature of the liquids with a candy thermometer to avoid any possible errors.

Sugar not only adds flavor to bread, it provides food for the yeast to grow. Sugar also aids in producing a nicely browned loaf. Coffee cake and sweet roll doughs usually have a higher proportion of sugar than do plain bread doughs.

Shortenings used in breads include butter, margarine, vegetable shortening, and cooking oil. They add flavor and help to make a more tender product. Like sugar, shortenings also aid in browning breads.

Liquids used in bread baking are usually milk and/or water. Milk adds extra nutrition and gives the bread a softer crust. Breads made with water are often crustier.

Eggs enhance the flavor, color, and texture of bread products. In addition, they are a nutritional bonus in bread.

Salt plays an important role, too. Not only does it contribute flavor, it is necessary to control the growth of the yeast.

Pretty enough for gift-giving

As soon as you take *Apricot-Topped Coffee Bread* (recipe on page 45) out of the oven, top it with a mixture of apricot preserves, honey, and nuts. Then, glaze with Confectioners' Icing.

Using an electric mixer makes mixing yeast-bread doughs easier. A mixer helps develop the gluten in flour, which lets bread hold its shape.

Kneading the dough properly and for a long enough period is an important step. On a lightly floured surface, knead till the dough is smooth.

PREPARATION HINTS

Mixing many of the yeast-bread doughs can be done, in part, with an electric mixer (1). Only the final amounts of flour need to be stirred in with a wooden spoon. Since a range of flour is given in most recipes, start with the smaller amount. Then, add flour until the dough is of the specified consistency.

Kneading is accomplished by turning out the yeast dough onto a lightly floured board or surface. Fold the dough over and push down with the heel of the hand, curving your fingers over the dough. Give the dough a quarter turn, then fold over and push down again (2). Knead, following this folding, pushing, and turning procedure, until the dough is smooth and elastic.

Rising of the dough occurs after you place the kneaded dough in a greased bowl (turn once to grease the surface), cover it with a towel, and place the dough in a warm place (3). Dough should double in bulk. The rising times given in the recipes are approximate; they depend on the temperature at which the dough rises. To tell when the dough has doubled, press two fingertips lightly ½ inch into the dough. If the indentation remains, the dough is ready for shaping (4).

Punch down the dough by pushing your fist into the center of the dough. Then, pull the edges of the dough to the center, turn dough over, and place on lightly floured surface.

To provide a warm place for the dough to rise, place dough on the top rack of a cold oven, and put a pan of hot water on the lower rack.

The dough has doubled and is ready to shape when you can lightly press two fingertips quickly ½ inch into dough and indentation remains.

Shaping a loaf of bread starts with dividing dough as specified in the recipe. Cover; let dough rest 10 minutes on a lightly floured surface. Then, roll dough into a 12 x 8-inch rectangle. Roll to the outer edges to remove all the bubbles (5). Roll up tightly, starting with the narrow edge. Seal with fingertips as you roll (6). Be sure to seal the final edge thoroughly. After rolling, seal the edge by pressing down on each end to make a thin sealed strip (7). Fold strips under loaf and place in greased baking pan or dish, folded ends down.

Test a bread for doneness by tapping the top crust with your finger (8). If there is a hollow sound, the bread is thoroughly baked. Remove bread from pan at once; cool on a wire rack.

Storing yeast breads properly is necessary to keep them fresh-tasting. Wrap the bread in foil or clear plastic wrap, or place in a plastic bag. Then, store in a cool, dry place. (Do not refrigerate baked yeast breads, since refrigerator storage causes bread to stale.) For longer storage, freeze cooled breads, tightly wrapped in moisture-vaporproof wrap. Thaw wrapped breads at room temperature, or warm them in a 250° to 300° oven. Frost breads after thawing.

High-altitude adjustments are often necessary because breads rise more quickly at higher altitudes. If you live in a high-altitude area, experiment by using smaller amounts of yeast, watching the rising carefully, and baking when dough tests for double in size.

Roll up the rectangle, starting with the narrow edge. Seal with your fingertips as you roll. Be sure to seal the final edge of the dough.

Seal the two ends of the roll by pressing down to make a thin sealed strip at each end. Fold the sealed strips under the loaf and place in dish.

Shape a loaf of bread by rolling the specified portion of the dough on a lightly floured surface into a rectangle of uniform thickness.

Test the baked loaf for doneness by tapping the top with your finger. A hollow sound means that the loaf is properly baked. Remove from pan.

PERFECT WHITE BREAD
(easy-mix method)

5¾ to 6¼ cups all-purpose flour
1 package active dry yeast
2¼ cups milk
2 tablespoons sugar
1 tablespoon shortening
2 teaspoons salt

In large mixer bowl combine *2½ cups* of the flour and the yeast. In saucepan heat together milk, sugar, shortening, and salt just till warm (115-120°), stirring constantly to melt shortening. Add to dry mixture in mixer bowl. Beat at low speed with electric mixer for ½ minute, scraping sides of bowl constantly. Beat the mixture 3 minutes at high speed.

By hand, stir in enough of the remaining flour to make a moderately stiff dough. Turn out onto a lightly floured surface and knead till smooth and elastic (8 to 10 minutes). Shape in a ball. Place dough in lightly greased bowl; turn once to grease surface. Cover; let rise in warm place until double (about 1¼ hours). Punch dough down; turn out on lightly floured surface. Divide dough in 2 portions.

Shape each in a smooth ball; cover and let rest 10 minutes. Shape in loaves; place in two greased 8½x4½x2½-inch loaf pans. Cover and let rise till double (45 to 60 minutes). Bake at 375° till done, about 45 minutes. If tops brown too fast, cover loosely with foil the last 15 minutes. Remove from pans; cool. Makes 2 loaves.

PERFECT WHITE BREAD
(conventional method)

1 package active dry yeast
¼ cup warm water (110°)
2 cups milk
2 tablespoons sugar
1 tablespoon shortening
2 teaspoons salt
5¾ to 6¼ cups all-purpose flour

Soften yeast in warm water. In saucepan combine milk, sugar, shortening, and salt. Heat till sugar dissolves. Cool to lukewarm. Stir in *2 cups* of the flour; beat well. Add the softened yeast; beat thoroughly until smooth. Add enough remaining flour to make a moderately stiff dough. Turn out onto a lightly floured surface and knead till smooth and elastic (8 to 10 minutes). Shape in a ball. Place in lightly greased bowl; turn once to grease surface. Cover; let rise in warm place until double (about 1¼ hours).

Punch dough down; turn out on lightly floured surface. Divide dough into 2 portions. Shape each into a smooth ball; cover and let rest 10 minutes. Shape in loaves; place in two greased 8½x4½x2½-inch loaf pans. Cover and let rise in warm place till double (45 to 60 minutes). Bake at 375° till done, about 45 minutes. If tops brown too fast, cover loosely with foil the last 15 minutes. Remove from pans; cool. Makes 2.

REFRIG-A-RISE WHITE BREAD

Prepare *Perfect White Bread* recipe, using either the easy-mix or conventional method.

After the dough has been shaped into loaves and placed in loaf pans, brush with melted butter. Cover loosely with clear plastic wrap. Refrigerate 3 to 24 hours. When ready to bake, remove bread from refrigerator, uncover, and let stand 20 minutes. Just before baking, puncture any surface bubbles with a wooden pick. Bake at 375° till done, about 45 minutes. After 30 minutes of baking, brush tops with butter. Remove from pans and cool. Makes 2 loaves.

MINIATURE BREAD LOAVES

Prepare *Perfect White Bread* recipe, using either the easy-mix or conventional method.

After the dough has doubled in the bowl, punch down and turn out onto a lightly floured surface. Divide dough into 8 portions. Shape each into a smooth ball; cover and let rest 10 minutes. Shape in loaves; place in eight greased 4½x2½x1½-inch loaf pans. Cover; let rise till double (30 to 45 minutes). Bake at 400° about 25 minutes. Remove from pans; cool. Makes 8.

Bread with that old-fashioned flavor

Choose the preparation method you prefer for →
Perfect White Bread. Whether you use the easy-mix or the conventional method, you'll turn out loaves of bread you'll be proud to serve.

BASIC ROLLS
(easy-mix method)

4½ to 5 cups all-purpose flour
2 packages active dry yeast
1 cup milk
½ cup sugar
½ cup shortening
2 teaspoons salt
3 eggs

In large mixer bowl combine *2 cups* of the flour and the yeast. In saucepan heat milk, sugar, shortening, and salt just till warm (115-120°), stirring constantly to melt shortening. Add to dry mixture in mixer bowl; add eggs. Beat at low speed with electric mixer for ½ minute, scraping sides of bowl constantly. Beat 3 minutes at high speed. By hand, stir in enough remaining flour to make a moderately stiff dough. Turn out on a lightly floured surface; knead till smooth and elastic (5 to 8 minutes). Shape into a ball. Place in lightly greased bowl; turn once to grease surface. Cover; let rise in warm place till double (1 to 1½ hours).

Punch dough down; turn out on lightly floured surface. Cover; let rest 10 minutes. Shape dough into rolls, following Roll-Shaping Ideas. Cover and let rise in a warm place till double (about 30 to 45 minutes). If desired, carefully brush with melted butter or margarine. Bake at 400° till done, 10 to 12 minutes. Remove from pans. Makes 2 to 3 dozen rolls.

BASIC ROLLS
(conventional method)

2 packages active dry yeast
½ cup sugar
½ cup shortening
½ cup milk
2 teaspoons salt
4½ to 5 cups all-purpose flour
3 eggs

Soften yeast in ½ cup *warm* water (110°). In saucepan combine sugar, shortening, milk, and salt. Heat, stirring till sugar dissolves. Place in large bowl; cool to lukewarm. Stir in *1½ cups* of the flour; beat well. Add softened yeast and eggs; beat thoroughly until smooth. Stir in enough remaining flour to make a moderately stiff dough. Turn out on a lightly floured surface and knead till smooth and elastic (5 to 8 minutes). Shape into a ball. Place in lightly greased bowl, turning once. Cover; let rise in warm place until double (1 to 1½ hours).

Punch dough down; turn out on lightly floured surface. Cover; let rest 10 minutes. Shape dough into rolls, following Roll-Shaping Ideas. Cover and let rise in warm place till double (about 30 to 45 minutes). If desired, carefully brush with melted butter or margarine. Bake at 400° till done, 10 to 12 minutes. Remove from pans. Makes 2 to 3 dozen rolls.

REFRIG-A-RISE ROLLS

Prepare *Basic Rolls* recipe, using either the easy-mix or conventional method.

After the dough has been kneaded and shaped into a ball, cover and let rest 20 minutes. Punch down and shape dough into Fantans, Cloverleaves, or Short-Cut Cloverleaves. Place rolls in prepared pans and brush with melted butter. Cover with oiled waxed paper, then with clear plastic wrap. Refrigerate 2 to 24 hours.

When ready to bake, remove rolls from refrigerator, uncover, and let stand 20 minutes. Just before baking, puncture any surface bubbles with a greased wooden pick. Bake at 375° for 12 to 15 minutes.

NO-KNEAD REFRIGERATOR ROLLS

In large mixer bowl combine 1½ cups all-purpose flour and 1 package active dry yeast. In saucepan heat 1¼ cups milk, ¼ cup sugar, ¼ cup shortening, and 1 teaspoon salt just till warm (115-120°), stirring constantly to melt shortening. Add to dry mixture in mixer bowl; add 1 egg. Beat mixture at low speed with electric mixer for ½ minute, scraping sides of bowl constantly. Beat 3 minutes at high speed. By hand, stir in 2 to 2¼ cups all-purpose flour, enough to make a soft dough.

Cover and refrigerate dough at least 2 hours or till needed. (Use within 3 to 4 days.) About 1½ to 2 hours before serving time, shape dough into Butterhorns, Cloverleaves, Short-Cut Cloverleaves, or Bowknots. Cover; let rise till double (1 to 1¼ hours). Bake at 400° for 9 to 10 minutes. Makes 2 to 3 dozen.

Roll-Shaping Ideas

Fantans: Divide dough for *Basic Rolls* into three equal pieces, and round each into a ball. Roll each ball to a 12x9-inch rectangle. Brush with melted butter or margarine. With a sharp knife, cut each rectangle of dough lengthwise into 6 strips, each 1½ inches wide (shown above). Pile all 6 strips of dough on top of one another; make ends even. With sharp knife, cut stacked strips into 1½-inch lengths, making 8 pieces (shown below). Place pieces, cut side down, in greased muffin pans (alternate direction of pieces to allow room to expand). Let rise and bake as directed. Makes 2 dozen.

Cloverleaves: Divide dough for *Basic Rolls* in eight equal pieces; shape each into nine 1-inch balls, making a total of 72 balls. Pull edges under, smoothing tops. Place 3 balls in each greased muffin pan, smooth side up. Makes 24.

Short-Cut Cloverleaves: Divide dough for *Basic Rolls* into 4 pieces; shape each into 6 balls, pulling edges under to smooth tops. Place one ball in each greased muffin pan, smooth side up. Using scissors dipped in flour, snip top in half; snip each again, making 4 points. Makes 24.

Butterhorns: Divide dough for *Basic Rolls* into three equal pieces, and round each into a ball. Roll each ball into a 12-inch circle. Brush with melted butter. Cut each circle into 12 wedges. To shape rolls, begin at wide end of wedge and roll toward point. Place point down, 2 to 3 inches apart, on greased baking sheet. Makes 36.

Parker House Rolls: Divide dough for *Basic Rolls* in half. Roll out each half ¼ inch thick. Cut with floured 2½-inch round cutter. Brush with melted butter. Make an off-center crease in each round. Fold in half so top overlaps slightly (large half folds over small half). Place 2 to 3 inches apart on greased baking sheet. Makes 36.

Bowknots: Divide dough for *Basic Rolls* into four equal pieces. Divide each fourth into eight pieces. On a lightly floured surface, roll each piece of dough into a pencillike strand, each about 9 inches long. Form a loose knot (pull strands gently before tieing knots if they shrink). Place 2 to 3 inches apart on greased baking sheet. Let rise and bake as directed. Makes 32.

Rosettes: Divide dough for *Basic Rolls* into four equal pieces. Divide each fourth into eight pieces. On a lightly floured surface, roll each piece into a pencillike strand, 12 inches long. Form into a loose knot, leaving two long ends. Tuck top end under roll. Bring bottom end up and tuck into center of roll. Place 2 to 3 inches apart on greased baking sheet. Makes 32.

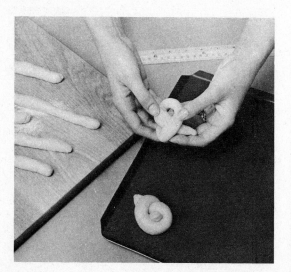

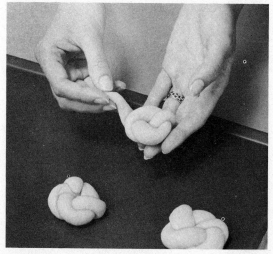

Corkscrews: Divide dough for *Basic Rolls* into six equal pieces. Divide each piece into six parts. On lightly floured surface, roll each piece into a strand 8 inches long. Wrap each piece around a greased wooden clothespin; seal ends. Place 2 to 3 inches apart on greased baking sheet. (Remove clothespin after baking.) Makes 36.

Swirls: Divide dough for *Basic Rolls* into six equal pieces. Divide each sixth into six pieces. On a lightly floured surface, roll each piece into a pencillike strand, 8 inches long. Beginning at center, make a loose swirl with each strand; tuck end under securely. Place 2 to 3 inches apart on greased baking sheet. Makes 36.

Stick Twists: Divide dough for *Basic Rolls* into three equal pieces, and round each into a ball. Roll each ball into a 14x6-inch rectangle. Brush with melted butter. Fold lengthwise into a 14x3-inch rectangle. Cut into strips 3 inches long and 1 inch wide. Twist each strip. Place 2 to 3 inches apart on greased baking sheet, pressing ends down on sheet. Makes 3½ dozen.

Circle Twists: Divide dough for *Basic Rolls* into three equal pieces, and round each into a ball. On a lightly floured surface, roll each ball into a 9x9-inch square. With a sharp knife, cut dough into strips 9 inches long and ¾ inch wide. Twist each strip and form into a circle; seal ends together. Place 2 to 3 inches apart on greased baking sheet. Makes 36.

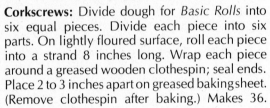

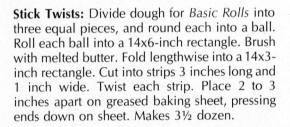

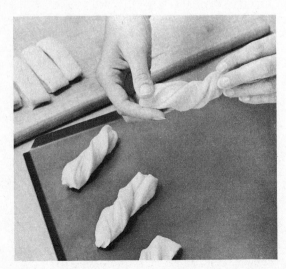

Bread and Roll Favorites

POTATO BREAD

> 1 medium potato, peeled and cubed
> 2 packages active dry yeast
> 2 tablespoons sugar
> 2 tablespoons shortening
> 6½ to 6¾ cups all-purpose flour

In saucepan cook potato in 1½ cups water till tender. Cool to lukewarm. Set aside ½ cup of the cooking liquid. Mash potato in the remaining liquid, adding water if needed, to make 2 cups potato mixture. Soften yeast in reserved ½ cup cooking liquid. Combine potato mixture, yeast mixture, sugar, shortening, and 1 tablespoon salt; mix well. Stir in *2 cups* of the flour; beat well. Let rise in warm place till double (about 45 minutes). Stir down; add enough remaining flour to make a moderately stiff dough. Turn out on floured surface; knead till smooth and elastic (about 10 minutes).

Shape into a ball. Place in greased bowl; turn once to grease surface. Cover; let rise until double (about 45 minutes). Punch down; turn out on lightly floured surface. Divide in half. Cover; let rest 10 minutes. Shape each into a loaf. Place in two greased 8½x4½x2½-inch loaf pans. Cover; let rise till almost double (about 45 minutes). If desired, brush tops lightly with milk and dust with flour. Bake at 375° for 40 to 45 minutes. Remove from pans; cool. Makes 2.

CHEESE BRAID

In large mixer bowl combine 2 cups all-purpose flour and 1 package active dry yeast. Heat 1½ cups milk, 2 tablespoons sugar, and 1½ teaspoons salt till warm (115-120°), stirring to dissolve sugar. Add to dry mixture in mixer bowl; add 1 egg and 2 cups shredded process pimiento cheese (8 ounces). Beat at low speed with mixer for ½ minute, scraping bowl. Beat 3 minutes at high speed. By hand, stir in 2½ to 3 cups all-purpose flour to make a stiff dough.

Knead on floured surface till smooth (8 to 10 minutes). Shape into ball. Place in greased bowl; turn once. Cover; let rise till double (about 1½ hours). Punch down; divide in 6 pieces. Cover; let rest 10 minutes. Roll each piece into a rope 15 inches long. On greased baking sheets, shape into 2 braids, using 3 ropes for each *(see tip, page 38)*. Cover; let rise till almost double (35 to 45 minutes). Bake at 375° for 15 to 20 minutes. Makes 2 braids.

SWEET BANANA BREAD

> 5½ to 6 cups all-purpose flour
> 2 packages active dry yeast
> ¾ cup milk
> ½ cup sugar
> ½ cup butter or margarine
> 2 ripe bananas, mashed (1 cup)
> 2 eggs

In large mixer bowl combine *2 cups* of the flour and the yeast. In saucepan heat milk, sugar, butter, and 1 teaspoon salt till warm (115-120°), stirring constantly to melt butter. Add to dry mixture in mixer bowl; add banana, 1 egg, and 1 egg yolk (reserve 1 egg white).

Beat at low speed with mixer for ½ minute, scraping bowl. Beat 3 minutes at high speed. By hand, stir in enough remaining flour to make a moderately stiff dough. Turn out on floured surface; knead till smooth (5 to 8 minutes). Place in greased bowl; turn once. Cover; let rise till double (about 1 hour). Punch down. Divide in half. Cover; let rest 10 minutes.

Shape into 2 round loaves. Place on greased baking sheets. Make vertical cuts about ⅛ inch deep around each loaf at ¾-inch intervals. Combine reserved egg white and 1 teaspoon water; brush tops. Let rise till double (30 to 45 minutes). Bake at 400° for 30 minutes. Makes 2.

Five yeast bread favorites

Choose from *Refrigerated Herb Rolls* (recipe on → page 34), *Potato Bread*, round *Sweet Banana Bread*, *Cheese Braid*, or *Two-Tone Bread* (recipe on page 21), a white-whole wheat combination.

Brushing tops of yeast breads

To achieve various types of yeast-bread crusts, brush in one of the following ways before baking. Brushing the bread carefully with melted shortening, butter, or cooking oil results in a tender, more browned crust. For crisp, shiny crusts, brush tops with milk, water, or egg diluted with milk or water. You can use egg whites, yolks, or the entire egg.

After baking, brush breads with melted butter to soften the crust and to enhance the color. If you want a crisp crust, omit brushing with butter.

PUMPKIN BREAD

   3¼ to 3½ cups all-purpose flour
    2 packages active dry yeast
   ½ teaspoon ground ginger
   ¼ teaspoon ground nutmeg
   ¼ teaspoon ground cloves
   ¾ cup milk
   ¼ cup packed brown sugar
    2 tablespoons butter or margarine
   1½ teaspoons salt
   ½ cup canned pumpkin
   ¾ cup raisins

In large mixer bowl thoroughly combine *1½ cups* of the flour, yeast, and spices. In saucepan heat milk, brown sugar, butter, and salt just till warm (115-120°), stirring constantly to melt butter. Add to dry mixture in mixer bowl; add pumpkin. Beat at low speed with electric mixer for ½ minute, scraping sides of bowl constantly. Beat 3 minutes at high speed. By hand, stir in raisins and enough of the remaining flour to make a moderately stiff dough. Turn out onto lightly floured surface and knead till smooth and elastic (5 to 8 minutes). Shape into ball.

Place in lightly greased bowl, turning once. Cover and let rise in warm place till double (about 1 hour). Punch down; cover and let rest 10 minutes. Shape into loaf; place in greased 8½x4½x2½-inch loaf pan. Cover; let rise till double (about 30 minutes). Bake at 375° for 35 to 40 minutes. Remove from pan; cool. Makes 1.

BACON BREAD

   3½ to 3¾ cups all-purpose flour
    1 package active dry yeast
   10 slices bacon
   1¼ cups milk
    1 tablespoon sugar
      Melted butter or margarine

In mixer bowl combine *1 cup* of the flour and the yeast. Cook bacon till crisp; drain, reserving 2 tablespoons drippings. Finely crumble bacon and set aside. Heat milk, reserved drippings, sugar, and 1 teaspoon salt till warm (115-120°), stirring constantly. Add to dry mixture. Beat at low speed with electric mixer for ½ minute, scraping bowl. Beat 3 minutes at high speed.

By hand, stir in crumbled bacon and enough remaining flour to make a moderately stiff dough. Turn out on lightly floured surface and knead till smooth and elastic (8 to 10 minutes). Shape into ball. Place in greased bowl; turn once. Cover; let rise till double (about 1¾ hours). Punch down; cover and let rest 10 minutes. Shape into loaf; place in greased 8½x4½x2½-inch loaf pan. Cover; let rise till double (35 to 40 minutes). Bake at 375° for 35 minutes. Brush with melted butter. Remove; cool. Makes 1 loaf.

HOT CROSS BREAD

In large mixer bowl combine 1½ cups all-purpose flour, 1 package active dry yeast, and ¼ teaspoon ground cinnamon. Heat ½ cup milk, ¼ cup sugar, ¼ cup shortening, and ½ teaspoon salt till warm (115-120°), stirring constantly. Add to dry mixture; add 2 eggs. Beat at low speed with electric mixer for ½ minute, scraping bowl.

Beat 3 minutes at high speed. Stir in 1½ to 2 cups all-purpose flour to make a moderately stiff dough. Stir in ¼ cup raisins and ¼ cup chopped mixed candied fruits. Knead on floured surface till smooth (8 to 10 minutes). Shape into ball. Place in greased bowl; turn once. Cover; let rise in warm place till double (1 to 1½ hours).

Punch down; cover and let rest 10 minutes. Shape into loaf; place in greased 9x5x3-inch loaf pan. Snip crosses down center. Cover; let rise till double (45 to 60 minutes). Bake at 350° about 30 minutes. Cover loosely with foil if over-browning occurs. Cool. Drizzle with Confectioners' Icing *(see page 26)*. Makes 1 loaf.

RAISIN-WHEAT BREAD

2¾ to 3 cups all-purpose flour
1 package active dry yeast
1¼ cups milk
2 tablespoons sugar
2 tablespoons light molasses
1 tablespoon butter or margarine
½ teaspoon salt
1 shredded wheat biscuit, finely
    crumbled (about ¾ cup)
1 cup raisins

In large mixer bowl combine *1½ cups* of the flour and the yeast. In saucepan heat *1 cup* of the milk, sugar, molasses, butter, and salt just till warm (115-120°), stirring constantly to melt butter. Combine shredded wheat and the remaining milk; let stand 2 to 3 minutes till softened. Add both milk mixtures to flour mixture in bowl.

Beat at low speed with electric mixer for ½ minute, scraping bowl constantly. Beat 3 minutes at high speed. By hand, stir in raisins and enough remaining flour to make a moderately stiff dough. Turn out onto floured surface and knead till smooth and elastic (8 to 10 minutes). Shape into ball. Place in lightly greased bowl, turning once to grease surface. Cover and let rise in warm place till almost double (50 to 60 minutes). Punch down; turn out on lightly floured surface. Cover and let rest 10 minutes. Shape into loaf and place in well-greased 8½x4½x2½-inch loaf pan. Cover; let rise till double (30 to 35 minutes). Bake at 375° till done, about 35 minutes. Remove from pan; cool. Makes 1 loaf.

TWO-TONE BREAD

5¼ to 5½ cups all-purpose flour
2 packages active dry yeast
3 cups milk
⅓ cup sugar
⅓ cup shortening
1 tablespoon salt
3 tablespoons dark molasses
2¼ cups whole wheat flour

In large mixer bowl combine *3 cups* of the all-purpose flour and the yeast. In saucepan heat together milk, sugar, shortening, and salt just till warm (115-120°), stirring constantly to melt shortening. Add to dry mixture in mixer bowl.

Beat at low speed with electric mixer for ½ minute, scraping sides of bowl constantly. Beat 3 minutes at high speed. Divide dough in half. To one half, stir in enough remaining all-purpose flour to make a moderately stiff dough. Turn out onto lightly floured surface and knead till smooth and elastic (5 to 8 minutes).

Shape into ball. Place in well-greased bowl, turning once; set aside. To remaining dough, stir in molasses and whole wheat flour. Turn out onto lightly floured surface. Knead till smooth and elastic (5 to 8 minutes), kneading in enough additional all-purpose flour (about 3 tablespoons) to make a moderately stiff dough. Shape into a ball. Place dough in well-greased bowl, turning once to grease surface.

Let both doughs rise in warm place until double (1 to 1¼ hours). Punch doughs down; cover and let rest 10 minutes. Roll out *half* the light dough and *half* the dark, each to a 12x8-inch rectangle. Place dark dough atop light; roll up tightly into loaf, beginning at short side. Repeat with remaining doughs. Place in two greased 8½x4½x2½-inch loaf pans. Cover; let rise till double (45 to 60 minutes). Bake at 375° for 30 to 35 minutes. Remove; cool. Makes 2.

For *Two-Tone Bread,* place dark portion of dough atop light dough. Roll up tightly, beginning at the short side. Form into a loaf; place in baking pan.

Grandma knew what she was doing when she served milk with *Grandma's Oatmeal Bread*. Besides being the perfect accompaniment, milk gives the cereal protein in the bread a nutritional boost.

GRANDMA'S OATMEAL BREAD

    2 packages active dry yeast
    ½ cup warm water (110°)
  1¼ cups boiling water
    1 cup quick-cooking rolled oats
    ½ cup light molasses
    ⅓ cup shortening
    1 tablespoon salt
  5¾ to 6 cups all-purpose flour
    2 beaten eggs
      Quick-cooking rolled oats
    1 beaten egg white
    1 tablespoon water

Soften yeast in the warm water. Combine boiling water, 1 cup rolled oats, molasses, shortening, and salt; cool to lukewarm. Stir in *2 cups* of the flour; beat well. Add the softened yeast and 2 beaten eggs; beat well. Stir in enough of the remaining flour to make a soft dough. Turn out onto a lightly floured surface and knead till smooth and elastic (8 to 10 minutes). Shape dough into a ball.

Place in lightly greased bowl, turning once to grease surface. Cover and let rise in warm place until double (about 1½ hours). Punch dough down; turn out on lightly floured surface. Divide dough in half. Cover and let rest 10 minutes. Coat two well-greased 8½x4½x2½-inch loaf pans with about 2 tablespoons rolled oats for each pan. Shape dough into loaves.

Place loaves in pans. Cover and let rise in warm place till double (45 to 60 minutes). Brush loaves with mixture of egg white and water; sprinkle tops lightly with rolled oats. Bake at 375° till done, about 40 minutes. Cover loosely with foil the last 15 minutes if tops are browning rapidly. Remove from pans and cool on wire racks. Makes 2 loaves.

ANADAMA BREAD

  5½ to 5¾ cups all-purpose flour
  2 packages active dry yeast
  ½ cup cornmeal
  ½ cup dark molasses
  ⅓ cup shortening
  1 tablespoon salt
  2 eggs
  Melted shortening

In large mixer bowl combine *3 cups* of the flour and the yeast. Very gradually stir cornmeal into 2 cups boiling water; add molasses, the ⅓ cup shortening, and salt. Cool to lukewarm. Combine cornmeal mixture and flour mixture; add eggs. Beat at low speed with electric mixer for ½ minute, scraping bowl constantly. Beat 3 minutes at high speed. By hand, stir in enough remaining flour to make a soft dough.

Turn out onto lightly floured surface and knead till smooth and elastic (7 to 10 minutes). Place in lightly greased bowl, turning once to grease surface. Cover and let rise in warm place till double (about 1½ hours). Punch down; divide in half. Cover; let rest 10 minutes. Shape in 2 loaves and place in greased 8½x4½x2½-inch loaf pans. Cover and let rise in warm place till double (45 to 60 minutes). Brush with melted shortening. Bake at 375° about 40 minutes. Cover with foil after 20 minutes if tops are getting too brown. Remove from pans; cool. Makes 2 loaves.

CORNMEAL LOAVES

These miniature loaves are pictured on page 6—

  6 to 6½ cups all-purpose flour
  2 packages active dry yeast
  2¼ cups milk
  ⅓ cup sugar
  ⅓ cup shortening
  1 tablespoon salt
  2 eggs
  1 cup yellow cornmeal
  Milk
  Yellow cornmeal

In large mixer bowl combine *3 cups* of the flour and the yeast. In saucepan heat 2¼ cups milk, sugar, shortening, and salt just till warm (115-120°), stirring constantly to melt shortening. Add to dry mixture in mixer bowl; add eggs. Beat at low speed with electric mixer for ½ minute, scraping bowl. Beat 3 minutes at high speed. By hand, stir in 1 cup cornmeal and enough remaining flour to make a soft dough.

Turn out onto lightly floured surface and knead till smooth and elastic (5 to 8 minutes). Shape into ball. Place in lightly greased bowl, turning once. Cover and let rise in warm place till double (1 to 1½ hours). Punch down; divide into eighths. Cover; let rest 10 minutes. Shape into 8 small loaves; place in 8 greased 6x3x2-inch loaf pans. (Or, divide dough in half and let rest. Shape into 2 loaves; place in two greased 9x5x3-inch loaf pans.) Cover; let rise in warm place till double (45 to 60 minutes). Brush tops with milk; sprinkle with cornmeal. Bake small loaves at 400° about 25 minutes, (Bake large loaves at 375° about 45 minutes.) Remove from pans; cool. Makes 8 small or 2 large loaves.

CHEESE LOAVES

  5½ to 5¾ cups all-purpose flour
  2 packages active dry yeast
  8 ounces sharp process American cheese, shredded (2 cups)
  2 cups milk
  2 tablespoons sugar
  2 tablespoons shortening

In large mixer bowl combine *2 cups* of the flour and the yeast. In saucepan heat cheese, milk, sugar, shortening, and 2 teaspoons salt just till warm (115-120°), stirring constantly to melt cheese. Add to dry mixture in mixer bowl. Beat at low speed with electric mixer for ½ minute, scraping bowl. Beat 3 minutes at high speed. By hand, stir in enough remaining flour to make a soft dough. Turn out onto lightly floured surface and knead till smooth and elastic (5 to 8 minutes). Shape into a ball.

Place in lightly greased bowl, turning once. Cover and let rise in warm place till double (45 to 60 minutes). Punch down; turn out on lightly floured surface. Divide in half. Cover and let rest 10 minutes. Shape into 2 loaves and place in two greased 8½x4½x2½-inch *or* 9x5x3-inch loaf pans. Cover and let rise in warm place till double (30 to 45 minutes). Bake at 375° till done, 30 to 35 minutes. Remove from pans and cool on wire racks. Makes 2 loaves.

...licing tips

...d bread knife is a useful tool ...g freshly baked loaves without ... them. Cool the bread slightly before attempting to slice, then slice loaves on a bread board, using a gentle sawing motion. Bread that's still warm is easier to slice if turned on its side. If you have en electric knife, use it to obtain clean slices quickly without squashing the loaf of bread.

OLD-TIME WHOLE WHEAT BREAD

    5 cups all-purpose flour
    2 packages active dry yeast
 2¾ cups water
    ½ cup packed brown sugar
    ¼ cup shortening
    1 tablespoon salt
    3 cups whole wheat flour

In large mixer bowl combine 3½ *cups* of the all-purpose flour and the yeast. In saucepan heat water, brown sugar, shortening, and salt just till warm (115-120°), stirring constantly to melt shortening. Add to dry mixture in mixer bowl. Beat at low speed with electric mixer for ½ minute, scraping sides of bowl constantly. Beat 3 minutes at high speed.

By hand, stir in the whole wheat flour and enough of the remaining all-purpose flour to make a moderately stiff dough. Turn out onto a lightly floured surface and knead till smooth and elastic (10 to 12 minutes). Shape into a ball. Place dough in a lightly greased bowl, turning once to grease surface. Cover and let rise in a warm place until double (about 1 hour).

Punch dough down; turn out onto lightly floured surface. Divide in half. Cover and let rest 10 minutes. Shape dough into two loaves and place in two greased 8½x4½x2½-inch loaf pans. Cover and let rise in a warm place until almost double (about 45 minutes). Bake at 375° for 40 to 45 minutes. If necessary, cover loosely with foil the last 20 minutes of baking to prevent overbrowning. Remove from pans and cool on wire racks. Makes 2 loaves.

PUMPERNICKEL BREAD

    3 packages active dry yeast
 2¾ cups rye flour
 2½ to 2¾ cups all-purpose flour
    ½ cup dark molasses
    2 tablespoons shortening
    1 tablespoon caraway seed
       Cornmeal

Soften yeast in 1½ cups *warm* water (110°). Combine rye flour, *1 cup* of the all-purpose flour, molasses, shortening, caraway seed, 1 tablespoon salt, and softened yeast; beat well. Stir in enough remaining all-purpose flour to make a stiff dough. Knead on lightly floured surface till smooth (8 to 10 minutes). Shape into ball. Place in greased bowl, turning once. Cover; let rise till double (about 1½ hours). Punch down.

Divide in half. Cover; let rest 10 minutes. Shape into 2 balls. Place on a greased baking sheet sprinkled with cornmeal. Cover; let rise till double (30 to 45 minutes). Bake at 375° till well browned, 30 to 35 minutes. For a chewy crust, brush with warm water several times during last 10 to 15 minutes of baking. Remove from baking sheet; cool. Makes 2 loaves.

RYE BREAD

In large mixer bowl combine 2½ cups all-purpose flour, 2 packages active dry yeast, and 1 tablespoon caraway seed. In saucepan heat 2 cups water, ½ cup packed brown sugar, 1 table-spoon shortening, and 1 teaspoon salt just till warm (115-120°), stirring constantly to melt shortening. Add to dry mixture in mixer bowl.

Beat at low speed with electric mixer for ½ minute, scraping sides of bowl constantly. Beat 3 minutes at high speed. By hand, stir in 2½ cups rye flour and ½ cup all-purpose flour to make a moderately stiff dough. Turn out onto lightly floured surface and knead till smooth and elastic. Shape into ball. Place in greased bowl, turning once. Cover and let rise in warm place till double (about 1½ hours). Punch down.

Divide in half. Cover; let rest 10 minutes. Shape in 2 round loaves; place on two greased baking sheets. Cover; let rise till double (about 40 minutes). Bake at 350° for 40 to 45 minutes. Cover with foil last 15 minutes if overbrowning occurs. Remove from sheets; cool. Makes 2.

HOME-FROZEN WHITE BREAD

6 to 6¼ cups all-purpose flour
3 packages active dry yeast
¼ cup sugar
2 tablespoons shortening

In large mixer bowl combine *2½ cups* of the flour and the yeast. Heat 2¼ cups water, sugar, shortening, and 2 teaspoons salt till warm (115-120°), stirring constantly to melt shortening. Add to dry mixture. Beat at low speed with mixer for ½ minute, scraping bowl. Beat 3 minutes at high speed. By hand, stir in enough remaining flour to make a moderately stiff dough.

Knead on floured surface till smooth (5 to 8 minutes). Cover; let rise till double (30 to 60 minutes). Divide in half; form into balls. Flatten each to 6 inches in diameter. Wrap and freeze. (Freeze up to 4 weeks at 0° or below.) Remove from freezer; place in greased bowl. Cover; let rise till double (3 to 3½ hours). Shape into 2 loaves; place in 2 greased 8½x4½x2½-inch loaf pans. Let rise till nearly double (45 to 60 minutes). Brush with butter. Bake at 375° for 30 to 35 minutes. Remove from pans. Makes 2.

FRENCH ONION BREAD

5½ to 6 cups all-purpose flour
2 packages active dry yeast
1 envelope dry onion soup mix
   (4- to 6-serving size)
2 tablespoons sugar
2 tablespoons shortening
   Cornmeal
1 beaten egg white

In large mixer bowl combine *2½ cups* of the flour and the yeast. Combine 2¼ cups water and soup mix; simmer, covered, for 10 minutes. Stir in sugar, shortening, and 1 teaspoon salt; cool well. Add to dry mixture. Beat at low speed with mixer for ½ minute, scraping bowl. Beat 3 minutes at high speed. Stir in enough remaining flour to make a moderately stiff dough.

Knead on floured surface till smooth (8 to 10 minutes). Shape into ball. Place in greased bowl; turn once. Cover; let rise in warm place till double (about 1 hour). Punch down; divide in half. Cover; let rest 10 minutes. Shape into 2 long loaves, tapering ends. Place on greased baking sheet sprinkled with cornmeal. Gash tops diagonally, ¼ inch deep. Cover; let rise till double (about 30 minutes). Bake at 375° for 20 minutes. Brush with mixture of egg white and 1 tablespoon water. Bake 10 to 15 minutes longer. Remove from baking sheet; cool. Makes 2.

HERB LOAF

In large mixer bowl combine 1½ cups all-purpose flour, 1 package active dry yeast, 2 teaspoons dried celery flakes, 2 teaspoons dried parsley flakes, and ½ teaspoon dried thyme, crushed. In saucepan heat 1 cup milk, 2 tablespoons sugar, 2 tablespoons shortening, and 2 teaspoons onion salt just till warm (115-120°), stirring constantly to melt shortening. Add to dry mixture; add 1 egg. Beat at low speed with electric mixer for ½ minute, scraping bowl.

Beat 3 minutes at high speed. By hand, stir in 1½ to 2 cups all-purpose flour to make a moderately soft dough. Knead on lightly floured surface till smooth (5 to 8 minutes). Shape into ball. Place in greased bowl, turning once. Cover; let rise in warm place till double (about 1 hour). Punch down; cover and let rest 10 minutes. Shape into a round loaf; place in greased 9-inch pie plate. Cover and let rise till double (30 to 45 minutes). Bake at 375° till done, 30 to 35 minutes. Remove from pan; cool. Makes 1 loaf.

MOLASSES-OAT BREAD

In large mixer bowl combine 3 cups all-purpose flour, 2 cups quick-cooking rolled oats, ¼ cup packed brown sugar, 2 packages active dry yeast, and 2 teaspoons salt. Heat 1 cup milk, ½ cup water, ½ cup shortening, and ¼ cup light molasses till warm (115-120°), stirring constantly. Add to dry mixture in mixer bowl; add 2 eggs.

Beat at low speed with mixer for ½ minute, scraping bowl. Beat 3 minutes at high speed. By hand, stir in 1¾ to 2 cups all-purpose flour to make a soft dough. Knead till smooth (4 to 5 minutes). Place in greased bowl; turn once. Cover; let rise till double (about 1½ hours). Punch down; divide in half. Shape into 2 loaves. Brush with water; roll in rolled oats. Place in 2 greased 8½x4½x2½-inch loaf pans. Cover; let rise till double (about 1 hour). Bake at 350° for 40 to 45 minutes. Makes 2.

Confectioners' Icing

Combine 1 cup sifted powdered sugar, ¼ teaspoon vanilla, and enough milk to make of drizzling consistency (about 1½ tablespoons). Ices 2 loaves.

Cool bread slightly before icing. A wire rack with waxed paper underneath works well and makes cleanup easy. From a spoon, drizzle icing back and forth across loaf. Or, spread with a spatula. Be sure to add nuts, fruits, or other decorations before icing sets.

FROSTED RAISIN LOAVES

Soften 2 packages active dry yeast in ½ cup *warm* water (110°). Combine 1½ cups raisins, ¼ cup sugar, ¼ cup milk, ¼ cup butter, and 1½ teaspoons salt. Heat till sugar dissolves. Cool to lukewarm. Turn into large bowl. Stir in ¾ cup all-purpose flour. Add softened yeast and 2 eggs; beat well. Stir in 3 to 3¼ cups all-purpose flour to make a moderately stiff dough. Knead on floured surface till smooth (5 to 8 minutes). Shape into ball. Place in greased bowl; turn once. Cover; let rise till double (45 to 60 minutes). Punch down; divide in half.

Cover; let rest 10 minutes. Shape into 2 loaves; place in 2 greased 7½x3½x2-inch loaf pans. Cover; let rise till double (about 30 minutes). Bake at 375° for 25 to 30 minutes. (If browning too fast, cover with foil last 10 minutes.) Remove from pans; cool. Frost with Confectioners' Icing (see tip above). Makes 2 loaves.

CINNAMON SWIRL LOAF

7 to 7½ cups all-purpose flour
2 packages active dry yeast
2 cups milk
½ cup sugar
½ cup shortening
2 teaspoons salt
2 eggs
• • •
½ cup sugar
2 teaspoons ground cinnamon
Confectioners' Icing (see tip)

In large mixer bowl combine *3½ cups* of the flour and the yeast. In saucepan heat milk, ½ cup sugar, shortening, and salt just till warm (115-120°), stirring constantly to melt shortening. Add to dry mixture in mixer bowl; add eggs. Beat at low speed with electric mixer for ½ minute, scraping sides of bowl constantly. Beat 3 minutes at high speed. By hand, stir in enough of the remaining flour to make a moderately soft dough. Turn out on lightly floured surface and knead till smooth and elastic (5 to 8 minutes). Shape into a ball. Place in lightly greased bowl, turning once to grease surface.

Cover; let rise in warm place till double (about 1 hour). Punch dough down; turn out on lightly floured surface. Divide in half. Cover; let rest 10 minutes. Roll *each half* into a 15x7-inch rectangle. Brush entire surface with water.

Combine the ½ cup sugar and the ground cinnamon. Spread each rectangle with *half* the sugar-cinnamon mixture. Roll dough up as for jelly roll, beginning with narrow side. Seal long edge and ends. Place, sealed edge down, in 2 greased 9x5x3-inch loaf pans. Cover and let rise in warm place till almost double (35 to 45 minutes). Bake at 375° till done, 35 to 40 minutes. (If crust browns too quickly, cover with foil last 15 minutes of baking.) Remove bread from pans and cool on wire racks. Drizzle with Confectioners' Icing. Makes 2 loaves.

A perfect breakfast treat

Make the swirl in *Cinnamon Swirl Loaf* by rolling → up a mixture of sugar and spice in the dough. After baking, drizzle Confectioners' Icing over top. This bread is delicious when toasted, too.

OATMEAL BATTER BREAD

In large mixer bowl combine 1½ cups all-purpose flour, 1 cup rolled oats, and 1 package active dry yeast. In saucepan heat 1¼ cups milk, ¼ cup shortening, ¼ cup honey, and 2 teaspoons salt just till warm (115-120°), stirring constantly to melt shortening. Add to dry mixture in mixer bowl. Add 1 egg and 1 egg yolk to mixture (reserve 1 egg white).

Beat at low speed with electric mixer for ½ minute, scraping sides of bowl constantly. Beat 3 minutes at high speed. By hand, stir in 1½ cups all-purpose flour to make a soft dough. Beat till smooth. Cover and let rise in a warm place till double (1¾ to 2 hours). Stir dough down. Sprinkle a greased 2-quart casserole with 2 tablespoons rolled oats. Turn dough into prepared casserole. Let rise in a warm place till double (about 45 minutes).

Brush with beaten, reserved egg white and sprinkle with 1 tablespoon rolled oats. Bake at 350° for 45 to 50 minutes. Let stand in dish 15 minutes. Remove from dish. Makes 1.

CHEESE CASSEROLE BREAD

2¼ cups all-purpose flour
¼ cup grated Parmesan cheese
2 tablespoons snipped parsley
1 package active dry yeast
¼ teaspoon baking soda
1 cup cream-style cottage cheese
⅓ cup water
2 tablespoons butter or margarine
1 egg

In large mixer bowl combine *1 cup* of the flour, Parmesan, parsley, yeast, and soda. Heat together the cottage cheese, water, and butter just till warm (115-120°), stirring constantly to melt butter. Add to dry mixture; add egg. Beat at low speed with electric mixer for ½ minute, scraping sides of bowl constantly. Beat 3 minutes at high speed. By hand, stir in remaining flour. Turn into greased bowl.

Cover; let rise till double (about 1½ hours). Stir down. Spread evenly in a greased 1½-quart casserole. Let rise till nearly double (about 40 minutes). Bake at 350° for 50 to 55 minutes. Cover top with foil if bread browns too quickly. Remove from casserole; cool. Makes 1 loaf.

EASY DILL-ONION BREAD

3 cups all-purpose flour
1 package active dry yeast
1¼ cups milk
2 tablespoons sugar
2 tablespoons butter or margarine
2 teaspoons dried dillseed
2 teaspoons instant minced onion
1 egg

In small mixer bowl combine *1½ cups* of the flour and the yeast. In saucepan heat milk, sugar, butter, dillseed, onion, and 1 teaspoon salt just till warm (115-120°), stirring constantly to melt butter. Add to dry mixture; add egg. Beat at low speed with electric mixer for ½ minute, scraping bowl. Beat 3 minutes at high speed. By hand, stir in remaining flour.

Cover; let rise till double (30 to 45 minutes). Stir down. Spread evenly in a greased 9x5x3-inch loaf pan. Let rise till nearly double (about 30 minutes). Bake at 350° for 25 to 30 minutes. Cover loosely with foil if bread browns too quickly. Remove from pan; cool. Makes 1 loaf.

GARDEN BATTER BREAD

3 cups all-purpose flour
1 package active dry yeast
1¼ cups warm water (110°)
¼ cup light molasses
2 tablespoons cooking oil
1 egg
1 cup wheat germ
1 cup coarsely grated carrot
¼ cup snipped parsley

In large mixer bowl combine *2 cups* of the flour, yeast, and 2 teaspoons salt. Add water, molasses, oil, and egg. Beat at low speed with electric mixer for ½ minute, scraping sides of bowl constantly. Beat mixture 3 minutes at high speed. By hand, stir in the remaining flour, wheat germ, grated carrot, and parsley. Turn batter into a greased 2-quart casserole.

Cover; let rise in warm place until nearly double (45 to 60 minutes). Bake at 350° for 50 to 60 minutes. Cover loosely with foil after the first 20 minutes of baking. Remove from casserole immediately. Brush top crust with melted butter, if desired. Cool. Makes 1 loaf.

If you're looking for a quick, easy yeast-leavened bread, try *English Muffin Bread*. The flavor of this casserole bread is similar to the familiar muffin.

PIZZA BATTER BREAD

    3 cups all-purpose flour
    1 package active dry yeast
    ½ teaspoon dried oregano, crushed
    ¼ teaspoon garlic powder
 1¼ cups water
    2 tablespoons butter or margarine
    1 tablespoon sugar
    1 teaspoon salt
    ¼ cup finely chopped pepperoni

In small mixer bowl combine *1½ cups* of the flour, yeast, oregano, and garlic powder. In saucepan heat water, butter, sugar, and salt just till warm (115-120°), stirring constantly to melt butter. Add to dry mixture in mixer bowl. Beat at low speed with electric mixer for ½ minute, scraping sides of bowl constantly.

Beat 3 minutes at high speed. By hand, stir in pepperoni and enough remaining flour to make a moderately soft dough. Cover; let rise till double (45 to 60 minutes). Stir down. Spread evenly in a greased 9x5x3-inch loaf pan. Let rise till double (about 30 minutes). Bake at 375° for 35 to 40 minutes. Remove from pan. Makes 1.

ENGLISH MUFFIN BREAD

 2½ to 3 cups all-purpose flour
    1 package active dry yeast
    1 tablespoon sugar
    Cornmeal

In large mixer bowl combine *1 cup* of the flour and the yeast. In saucepan heat 1¼ cups water, sugar, and ¾ teaspoon salt till warm (115-120°), stirring to dissolve sugar. Add to dry mixture in bowl. Beat at low speed with electric mixer for ½ minute, scraping bowl. Beat 3 minutes at high speed. By hand, stir in enough remaining flour to make a soft dough. Shape into ball.

Place in lightly greased bowl; turn once to grease surface. Cover; let rise until double (about 1 hour). Punch down. Cover; let rest 10 minutes. Grease a 1-quart casserole; sprinkle with cornmeal. Place dough in casserole; sprinkle top with cornmeal. Cover; let rise till double (30 to 45 minutes). Bake at 400° for 40 to 45 minutes. Cover loosely with foil if top browns too quickly. Remove from dish; cool. Makes 1.

RYE ROUND BREAD

 1½ cups rye flour
 2¼ cups all-purpose flour
    1 package active dry yeast
    1 tablespoon caraway seed
    1 teaspoon salt
 1¼ cups warm water (110°)
    2 tablespoons cooking oil
    2 tablespoons honey

In large mixer bowl combine rye flour, ½ *cup* of the all-purpose flour, yeast, caraway seed, and salt. Combine the water, oil, and honey. Add to dry mixture in mixer bowl. Beat at low speed with electric mixer for ½ minute, scraping sides of bowl constantly. Beat 3 minutes at high speed. By hand, stir in remaining all-purpose flour. Place in lightly greased bowl; turn once. Cover; let rise in warm place till double (about 1 hour). Stir down. Spread evenly in well-greased 1½-quart casserole. Let rise till nearly double (about 30 minutes). Bake at 375° for 45 to 50 minutes. Cover top with foil if bread browns too quickly. Remove from dish. Makes 1.

ONION ROLLS

In large mixer bowl combine 2½ cups all-purpose flour and 2 packages active dry yeast. Heat 2¼ cups milk, 2 tablespoons sugar, 2 tablespoons instant minced onion, 2 tablespoons cooking oil, 1 tablespoon prepared mustard, 1½ teaspoons salt, and ¼ teaspoon pepper just till warm (115-120°), stirring constantly. Add to dry mixture in mixer bowl; add 1 egg. Beat at low speed with electric mixer for ½ minute, scraping bowl. Beat 3 minutes at high speed.

By hand, stir in 3½ cups all-purpose flour to make a moderately stiff dough. Knead on floured surface till smooth and elastic (about 5 minutes). Shape into a ball. Place in greased bowl, turning once. Cover; let rise in warm place till double (45 to 60 minutes). Punch down; divide dough in half. Divide each half in 9 portions. Cover and let rest 10 minutes. Shape into balls and flatten to 3½-inch circles. Place on greased baking sheets. Let rise till double (20 to 30 minutes). Combine ¼ cup water and 2 tablespoons instant minced onion; let stand 5 minutes. Combine 1 beaten egg and 2 tablespoons water; brush onto rolls. Sprinkle with onion mixture. Bake at 375° for 20 to 25 minutes. Remove from baking sheets. Makes 18.

BAGELS

   4¼ to 4½ cups all-purpose flour
   2 packages active dry yeast
   1½ cups warm water (110°)
   3 tablespoons sugar
   1 tablespoon salt

In large mixer bowl combine *1½ cups* of the flour and the yeast. Combine water, sugar, and salt. Add to dry mixture in mixer bowl. Beat at low speed with electric mixer for ½ minute, scraping sides of bowl constantly. Beat 3 minutes at high speed. By hand, stir in enough of the remaining flour to make a moderately stiff dough. Turn out onto lightly floured surface and knead till smooth and elastic (8 to 10 minutes). Cover; let dough rest 15 minutes.

Cut into 12 portions; shape into smooth balls. Punch a hole in center of each with a floured finger. Pull gently to enlarge hole, working each bagel into uniform shape. Cover; let rise 20 minutes. (Optional step for glossy, smooth sur-

face: Place raised bagels on greased baking sheet and broil 5 inches from heat for 1½ to 2 minutes on each side.)

In large kettle combine 1 gallon water and 1 tablespoon sugar; bring to boiling. Reduce heat to simmering; cook 4 or 5 bagels at a time for 7 minutes, turning once. Drain. Place on greased baking sheet. Bake at 375° for 30 to 35 minutes. (For bagels that have been broiled, bake about 25 minutes.) Makes 12.

Onion Bagels: Prepare Bagels as above, *except* cook ½ cup finely chopped onion in 3 tablespoons butter or margarine till tender but not brown. Brush onion-butter mixture over tops of bagels after first 15 minutes of baking.

Herb Bagels: Prepare Bagels as above, *except* combine 2 teaspoons dried marjoram, crushed, *or* 1 teaspoon dried dillweed, crushed, with the flour and yeast mixture.

WHOLE WHEAT BAGELS

   2¾ to 3 cups all-purpose flour
   2 packages active dry yeast
   1½ cups warm water (110°)
   3 tablespoons sugar
   1 tablespoon salt
   1¼ cups whole wheat flour

In large mixer bowl combine *1½ cups* of the all-purpose flour and the yeast. Combine water, sugar, and salt. Add to dry mixture. Beat at low speed with electric mixer for ½ minute, scraping bowl constantly. Beat 3 minutes at high speed. By hand, stir in the whole wheat flour and enough remaining all-purpose flour to make a moderately stiff dough. Turn out on a lightly floured surface and knead till smooth (8 to 10 minutes). Cover; let rest 15 minutes.

Cut into 12 portions; shape each portion into a smooth ball. Punch a hole in center of each with a floured finger. Pull gently to enlarge hole, working each bagel into uniform shape. Cover; let rise 20 minutes. In large kettle, combine 1 gallon water and 1 tablespoon sugar; bring to boiling. Reduce heat to simmering; cook 4 or 5 bagels at a time for 7 minutes, turning once. Drain. Place on greased baking sheet. Bake at 375° for 30 to 35 minutes. Remove from baking sheet; cool. Makes 12 bagels.

Tug at a chewy, warm-from-the-oven *Bagel* spread with creamy butter, and experience a new bread delight. Or drizzle honey atop the golden rolls, or sandwich with cream cheese and smoked salmon.

Shape bagel dough into smooth balls. Punch a hole in center with floured finger. Pull to enlarge hole, working bagels into uniform shape.

Boiling the raised dough in sugared water for a few minutes before baking makes bagels chewy. Use tongs to turn them, and drain on towels.

CRUSTY RYE ROLLS

4 cups rye flour
2 packages active dry yeast
2 tablespoons caraway seed
2 cups milk
½ cup sugar
3 tablespoons shortening
2 eggs
3 cups all-purpose flour

In large mixer bowl combine *3 cups* rye flour, yeast, and caraway. Heat milk, sugar, shortening, and 1 tablespoon salt till warm (115-120°), stirring constantly to melt shortening. Add to dry mixture; add eggs. Beat at low speed with mixer for ½ minute, scraping bowl. Beat 3 minutes at high speed. Stir in remaining rye flour and enough all-purpose flour to make a moderately stiff dough. Knead on floured surface till smooth (10 minutes). Shape into ball.

Place in greased bowl; turn once. Cover; let rise till double (about 1 hour). Punch down; shape into 24 oval rolls. Place on greased baking sheet. Cover; let rise till double (about 30 minutes). Brush with water; sprinkle with coarse salt and caraway seed, if desired. Bake at 375° for 15 to 20 minutes. Makes 24.

CORNMEAL BUNS

In large mixer bowl combine 3 cups all-purpose flour and 1 package active dry yeast. In saucepan heat 2¼ cups milk, ½ cup sugar, ½ cup butter, and 1 teaspoon salt just till warm (115-120°), stirring constantly to melt butter. Add to dry mixture in mixer bowl; add 2 eggs.

Beat at low speed of mixer for ½ minute, scraping bowl. Beat 3 minutes at high speed. At low speed, beat in 1½ cups cornmeal. By hand, stir in 2½ to 3 cups all-purpose flour to make a moderately stiff dough. Turn out on floured surface; knead till smooth and elastic (6 to 8 min-

Great rolls to serve with salads

← Complete the meal with freshly baked rolls or breadsticks. Pass *Crusty Rye Rolls*, topped with salt and caraway seed, *Hurry-Up Cheese Buns*, or *Barbecue Breadsticks* (recipe on page 35).

utes). Place in greased bowl, turning grease surface. Cover; let rise in warm pla double (1 to 1¼ hours).

Punch down; turn out onto lightly floure surface. Shape into 72 balls. Place 2 balls in each greased 2½-inch muffin pan. Cover; let rise till nearly double (50 to 60 minutes). Bake at 375° for 12 to 15 minutes. Makes 36.

CRUSTY WATER ROLLS

1 package active dry yeast
2 tablespoons shortening
1 tablespoon sugar
3¼ to 3½ cups all-purpose flour
2 slightly beaten egg whites

Soften yeast in ¼ cup *warm* water (110°). Combine ¾ cup *boiling* water, shortening, sugar, and 1½ teaspoons salt; stir till shortening melts. Cool to lukewarm. Stir in *1 cup* flour; beat well. Add yeast and egg whites; beat well. Stir in enough flour to make a soft dough. Turn out onto floured surface; knead till smooth (about 10 minutes). Shape into a ball. Place in greased bowl; turn once. Cover; let rise in warm place till double (about 1 hour). Punch down. Turn out. Cover; let rest 10 minutes.

Shape into 18 round rolls. Place 2½ inches apart on greased baking sheet. Cover; let rise till double (about 45 minutes). Place large, shallow pan on bottom oven rack; fill with boiling water. Bake rolls on rack above water at 450° for 10 to 12 minutes. Makes 18.

HURRY-UP CHEESE BUNS

In mixer bowl combine 1 cup all-purpose flour and 1 package active dry yeast. Heat one 5-ounce jar sharp process American cheese spread, ½ cup water, ¼ cup shortening, 2 tablespoons sugar, and 1 teaspoon salt just till warm (115-120°), stirring constantly to melt shortening. Add to dry mixture; add 1 egg. Beat at low speed with electric mixer for ½ minute, scraping bowl. Beat 3 minutes at high speed. By hand, stir in 1 cup all-purpose flour. Turn out onto floured surface. Shape into 12 rolls; place in well-greased muffin pans. Let rise till nearly double (1 to 1½ hours). Bake at 350° for 15 to 18 minutes. Remove from pans; cool. Makes 12.

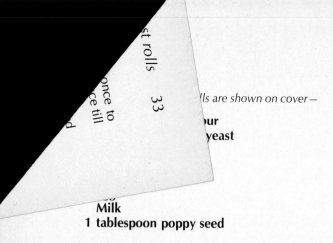

lls are shown on cover —

ur

yeast

Milk
1 tablespoon poppy seed

In large mixer bowl combine *2 cups* of the flour and the yeast. Heat milk, shortening, sugar, and 1 teaspoon salt till warm (115-120°), stirring constantly to melt shortening. Add to dry mixture in mixer bowl; add egg. Beat at low speed with electric mixer for ½ minute, scraping bowl. Beat 3 minutes at high speed. At low speed, beat in remaining flour till batter is smooth, about 2 minutes. (Since batter is stiff, use rubber spatula to push it away from beaters.)

Cover; let rise in warm place till double (about 1 hour). Stir down and beat thoroughly with wooden spoon. Let rest 5 minutes. Drop batter by tablespoons into greased muffin pans, filling half full. Cover; let rise till double (about 30 minutes). Brush tops lightly with milk; sprinkle with poppy seed. Bake at 400° till done, 12 to 15 minutes. Makes 20 rolls.

HAMBURGER BUNS

In large mixer bowl combine 4 cups all-purpose flour and 2 packages active dry yeast. Combine 2 cups *warm* water (110°), ¾ cup cooking oil, ½ cup sugar, and 1 tablespoon salt. Add to mixture in bowl; add 3 eggs. Beat at low speed with mixer for ½ minute, scraping bowl. Beat 3 minutes at high speed. By hand, stir in 4 cups all-purpose flour to make a soft dough.

Turn out on floured surface; knead till smooth and elastic. Place in greased bowl, turning once. Cover; let rise in warm place till double (about 1 hour). Punch down; divide dough in 3 portions. Cover; let rest 5 minutes. Divide each portion into 8 balls. Turn ball in hands, folding edges under to make even circle. Press ball flat between hands. Place on greased baking sheets, pressing to 3½-inch circles. Let rise till double (about 30 minutes). Bake at 375° about 10 minutes. Makes 24 buns.

WHOLE WHEAT ROLLS

These textured rolls are pictured on page 6 —

  3½ **cups whole wheat flour**
    2 **packages active dry yeast**
    2 **cups milk**
  ½ **cup sugar**
    3 **tablespoons shortening**
    1 **tablespoon salt**
    2 **eggs**
    3 **to 3½ cups all-purpose flour**

In large mixer bowl combine whole wheat flour and yeast. Heat milk, sugar, shortening, and salt just till warm (115-120°), stirring constantly to melt shortening. Add to dry mixture; add eggs. Beat at low speed with electric mixer for ½ minute, scraping bowl. Beat 3 minutes at high speed. By hand, stir in enough all-purpose flour to make a moderately stiff dough.

Turn out on floured surface; knead till smooth. Place in greased bowl; turning once. Cover; let rise till double (about 1½ hours). Punch down; cover and let rest 10 minutes. Shape into 24 rolls; place on greased baking sheets. Cover; let rise till almost double (about 45 minutes). Bake at 400° for 15 to 20 minutes. Makes 24.

REFRIGERATED HERB ROLLS

Herb-flavored cloverleafs are shown on page 19 —

In large mixer bowl combine 1½ cups all-purpose flour, 1 package active dry yeast, 2 teaspoons celery seed, and 1 teaspoon dried thyme, crushed. In saucepan heat together 1¼ cups milk, ¼ cup sugar, ¼ cup shortening, and 1 teaspoon salt just till warm (115-120°), stirring constantly to melt shortening. Add to dry mixture in mixer bowl; add 1 egg. Beat at low speed with electric mixer for ½ minute, scraping sides of bowl constantly. Beat 3 minutes at high speed. By hand, stir in 1¾ to 2 cups all-purpose flour to make a moderately soft dough. Place dough in greased bowl, turning once to grease surface. Cover and chill at least 2 hours.

Divide dough into fifty-four 1¼-inch balls. Place three balls in each compartment of greased muffin pans. Brush with a little melted butter or margarine. Let rise in warm place until double (about 1 hour). Bake at 400° for 12 to 15 minutes. Remove from muffin pans and cool on wire racks. Makes 18 rolls.

Warming yeast rolls

Warm yeast rolls in a brown paper bag for a fresh, just-baked flavor. Place rolls in the bag, sprinkle bag with water (a clothes sprinkler is a handy gadget), and fold the opening closed. Warm the rolls at 325° till heated through, about 10 minutes. You can wrap and heat the rolls in foil, too. Sprinkle rolls with water before wrapping.

If you have a microwave oven, use it to heat rolls in seconds. Place rolls on a paper napkin or plate to absorb moisture. Heat 1 roll about 10 to 15 seconds; 2 rolls, about 15 to 20 seconds; or 4 rolls, about 25 to 30 seconds.

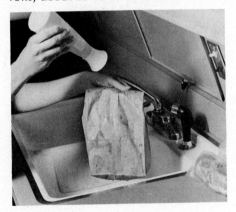

ITALIAN BREADSTICKS

    2 to 2¼ cups all-purpose flour
    1 package active dry yeast
    1 tablespoon sugar
    2 tablespoons olive or cooking oil
    1 egg yolk
    1 egg white

In large mixer bowl combine *1 cup* of the flour, yeast, sugar, and 1½ teaspoons salt. Combine ¾ cup *warm* water (110°), oil, and egg yolk. Add to dry mixture in mixer bowl. Beat at low speed with electric mixer for ½ minute, scraping bowl. Beat 3 minutes at high speed. By hand, stir in enough remaining flour to make a soft dough. Turn out on lightly floured surface; knead till smooth and elastic (5 to 8 minutes). Shape into a ball. Place in lightly greased bowl; turn once. Cover; refrigerate 3 to 4 hours or overnight.

Turn out on a very lightly floured surface and divide dough into 16 equal parts. Cover; let rest 10 minutes. Roll each piece of dough under hands to form a pencillike rope 14 inches long and ⅜ inch in diameter. Smooth each rope as you work. Place ropes 2 inches apart on greased baking sheet. Add 1 tablespoon water to egg white; beat till frothy. Brush egg mixture over dough. Let rise in a warm place till double (45 to 60 minutes). Brush again with egg mixture; sprinkle with coarse salt, if desired. Bake at 425° about 10 minutes. Makes 16.

BARBECUE BREADSTICKS

These crisp breadsticks are shown on page 32 —

    2½ to 3 cups all-purpose flour
    1 package active dry yeast
    ¾ cup milk
    ¼ cup bottled barbecue sauce
    2 tablespoons shortening
    1 tablespoon instant minced onion
    1 tablespoon sugar
    1 teaspoon salt
    1 egg

In large mixer bowl combine *1½ cups* of the flour and the yeast. In saucepan heat milk, barbecue sauce, shortening, onion, sugar, and salt just till warm (115-120°), stirring constantly to melt shortening. Add to dry mixture in mixer bowl; add egg. Beat at low speed with electric mixer for ½ minute, scraping sides of bowl constantly. Beat 3 minutes at high speed. By hand, stir in enough of the remaining flour to make a stiff dough. Shape into a ball.

Place in lightly greased bowl, turning once to grease surface. Cover; let rise in warm place until double (1 to 1½ hours). Punch dough down; turn out on lightly floured surface. Divide into four portions. Cover and let rest 10 minutes. Divide each portion of dough into 8 pieces. Roll each piece under hands to form a pencillike rope 8 inches long. Smooth each rope as you work. Place on greased baking sheet. Cover and let rise in warm place till double (about 30 minutes). Bake at 400° till golden brown, 12 to 15 minutes. Remove from baking sheet; cool on wire racks. Makes 32.

Tasty Coffee Cakes

CINNAMON CRESCENTS

This coffee cake is pictured on page 2 —

4½ to 4¾ cups all-purpose flour
1 package active dry yeast
¾ cup milk
⅓ cup sugar
6 tablespoons butter or margarine
½ teaspoon salt
3 eggs
• • •
1 cup raisins
½ cup sugar
½ cup chopped walnuts
2 tablespoons butter, melted
1 teaspoon ground cinnamon
Confectioners' Icing (see page 26)

In large mixer bowl combine 2½ *cups* of the flour and the yeast. In saucepan heat milk, ⅓ cup sugar, 6 tablespoons butter or margarine, and salt just till warm (115-120°), stirring constantly to melt butter. Add to dry mixture in mixer bowl; add eggs. Beat at low speed with electric mixer for ½ minute, scraping sides of bowl constantly. Beat 3 minutes at high speed. By hand, stir in enough of the remaining flour to make a soft dough. Turn out on a lightly floured surface and knead till dough is smooth and elastic (8 to 10 minutes).

Shape into a ball. Place in lightly greased bowl, turning once to grease surface. Cover; let rise in warm place until double (about 1 hour). Punch dough down; turn out on lightly floured surface. Divide in half. Cover; let rest 10 minutes. Roll each half into a 12x10-inch rectangle. Combine raisins, ½ cup sugar, walnuts, 2 tablespoons butter, and cinnamon; sprinkle half over each rectangle. Roll as for jelly roll, starting with long edge; seal.

Place, sealed side down, on greased baking sheet, curving to form crescent and pinching ends to seal. Cover and let rise in warm place till double (about 30 minutes). Bake at 375° about 25 minutes. Cover with foil last 15 minutes to prevent overbrowning. Frost with Confectioners' Icing, and sprinkle with additional chopped walnuts, if desired. Makes 2 crescents.

CHERRY LATTICE COFFEE CAKE

1 package active dry yeast
¼ cup warm water (110°)
¾ cup butter or margarine
⅓ cup sugar
1 teaspoon salt
• • •
4 eggs
4 cups all-purpose flour
¾ cup light cream
• • •
Cherry Filling
¼ cup all-purpose flour
1 teaspoon water

Soften active dry yeast in the warm water. In mixer bowl cream together butter or margarine, sugar, and salt. Add 3 eggs and 1 egg yolk, one at a time, to creamed mixture, beating well after each addition. (Reserve 1 egg white.) Stir in 4 cups all-purpose flour alternately with the softened yeast and light cream. Mix, but do not beat. Set aside 1 cup of the dough and spread the remainder in 2 well-greased 9x9x2-inch baking pans. Cover both dough squares in each pan with Cherry Filling.

For lattice top, blend ¼ cup all-purpose flour into reserved dough. Roll out on floured surface to a 9-inch square. Cut into 16 strips. Arrange 8 strips in lattice pattern over Cherry Filling in each pan. Beat together reserved egg white and water; brush over strips of dough. Cover and let rise in warm place till double (1 to 1¼ hours). Bake at 375° for 20 to 25 minutes. Makes 2 coffee cakes.

Cherry Filling: Combine ¾ cup cherry preserves, ½ cup softened butter, ½ cup chopped almonds, and ½ cup sugar. Mix well.

Fanciful crisscross coffee treat

Serve one *Cherry Lattice Coffee Cake* to your → morning coffee friends, and save the second one to treat your family. The recipe bonus is two scrumptious coffee cakes from one recipe.

Braiding coffee cakes

Braiding gives an unusual twist to coffee cakes. It's also fun and easy to do. Simply divide dough in thirds and shape into balls. Form each ball into a long rope, the length specified in the recipe. Line up the 3 ropes, 1 inch apart, on a greased baking sheet. Braid loosely, beginning in middle and working toward ends. Pinch ends and tuck under.

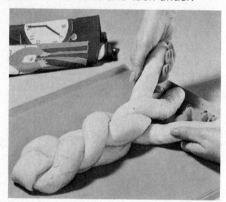

QUICK COFFEE CAKE

2 cups all-purpose flour
1 package active dry yeast
½ cup milk
6 tablespoons butter or margarine
5 tablespoons sugar
1 egg
⅓ cup slivered almonds
1 tablespoon butter or margarine

In large mixer bowl combine *1 cup* of the flour and the yeast. Heat milk, 6 tablespoons butter, *4 tablespoons* of the sugar, and ½ teaspoon salt till warm (115-120°). Add to dry mixture; add egg. Beat at low speed with mixer for ½ minute, scraping bowl. Beat 3 minutes at high speed. By hand, stir in enough remaining flour to make a soft dough. Turn into a greased 8x1½- or 9x1½-inch round baking pan. Sprinkle with nuts and 1 tablespoon sugar. Cover; let rise till almost double (about 1 hour). Dot with butter. Bake at 375° for 18 to 20 minutes. Makes 1.

LEMON-POPPY SEED BRAID

In large mixer bowl combine 1 cup all-purpose flour and 2 packages active dry yeast. In saucepan heat ½ cup water, ¼ cup sugar, ¼ cup butter or margarine, and ½ teaspoon salt just till warm (115-120°), stirring to melt butter. Add to dry mixture; add 1 egg and 1 tablespoon grated lemon peel. Beat at low speed with electric mixer for ½ minute, scraping sides of bowl constantly. Beat 3 minutes at high speed. By hand, stir in 2 cups all-purpose flour to make a moderately soft dough. Turn out on lightly floured surface and knead till smooth and elastic (8 to 10 minutes). Shape into a ball. Place in lightly greased bowl, turning once. Cover; let rise in warm place until double (about 1½ hours).

Punch dough down; turn out on lightly floured surface. Divide in thirds. Cover; let rest 10 minutes. Roll each portion into a 16x4-inch rectangle. Spread each with one-third of the Raisin-Poppy Seed Filling; roll and seal edge. Line up the 3 ropes, 1 inch apart, on greased baking sheet. Braid loosely *(see braiding tip at left)*; pinch ends together and tuck under. Cover and let rise in warm place till double (about 45 minutes). Bake at 375° for 20 to 25 minutes. Cover with foil last 15 minutes. Drizzle warm braid with Lemon Icing. Makes 1 braid.

Raisin-Poppy Seed Filling: Blend ½ of 8-ounce can poppy seed filling, ¼ cup light raisins, and 1½ teaspoons grated lemon peel.

Lemon Icing: Mix together 1 cup sifted powdered sugar, 1 tablespoon milk, and 1½ teaspoons lemon juice.

MORAVIAN COFFEE CAKE

Prepare instant mashed potatoes (enough for 1 serving) according to package directions. Soften yeast from one 13¾-ounce package hot roll mix in ¾ cup *warm* water (110°). Stir in 1 egg and mashed potatoes; mix well. Add flour mixture from mix; beat well. Cover and let rise till double (about 45 minutes). Stir down; spread evenly in greased 9x9x2-inch baking pan. Let rise till double (about 30 minutes). With finger, gently make indentations in top of bread at 1½-inch intervals. Drizzle ¼ cup melted butter over. Combine ½ cup packed brown sugar and ½ teaspoon ground cinnamon; sprinkle atop. Bake at 400° for 20 to 25 minutes. Serves 8.

Pour the coffee, then pass cinnamon- and nut-flavored *Spicy Prune Ring* around the table, letting each person break off a piece from the ring. Each tender roll is filled with a mouth-watering prune filling.

SPICY PRUNE RING

    3 to 3¼ cups all-purpose flour
    1 package active dry yeast
    ¾ cup milk
    ⅓ cup sugar
    ¼ cup butter or margarine
    ½ teaspoon salt
    1 egg
    ½ of 8-ounce can prune filling (½ cup)
    ⅓ cup sugar
    ⅓ cup finely chopped almonds, toasted
    1 teaspoon ground cinnamon
    ¼ cup butter or margarine, melted

In large mixer bowl combine *1½ cups* of the flour and the yeast. Heat milk, ⅓ cup sugar, ¼ cup butter, and salt till warm (115-120°), stirring to melt butter. Add to dry mixture in mixer bowl; add egg. Beat at low speed with electric mixer for ½ minute, scraping bowl. Beat 3 minutes at high speed. By hand, stir in enough remaining flour to make a soft dough. Turn out on a lightly floured surface and knead till smooth and elastic (8 to 10 minutes). Shape into a ball. Place in lightly greased bowl, turning once. Cover; let rise till double (about 1 hour).

Punch dough down; turn out on lightly floured surface. Cover; let rest 10 minutes. Roll to a 15x9-inch rectangle. Cut dough into fifteen 3-inch squares. Place about 2 teaspoons filling in center of each. Bring opposite corners of dough together, forming a small square; pinch edges together to seal. In small bowl combine ⅓ cup sugar, almonds, and cinnamon. Dip prune-filled rolls in melted butter, then in sugar-almond mixture. Stand rolls on edge, side by side, in greased 9-inch tube pan. Cover; let rise till double (about 45 minutes). Bake at 375° for 30 to 35 minutes. Cool in pan. Makes 1.

RHUBARB KUCHEN

3¾ cups all-purpose flour
1 package active dry yeast
1 cup milk
6 tablespoons butter or margarine
⅓ cup sugar
½ teaspoon salt
2 eggs
1½ cups sugar
2 teaspoons ground cinnamon
1 beaten egg yolk
⅓ cup light cream
3 cups thinly sliced rhubarb
(about 1 pound)

In large mixer bowl combine *2 cups* of the flour and the yeast. In saucepan heat milk, butter, ⅓ cup sugar, and salt just till warm (115-120°), stirring constantly to melt butter. Add to dry mixture in mixer bowl; add eggs. Beat at low speed with electric mixer for ½ minute, scraping sides of bowl constantly. Beat 3 minutes at high speed. By hand, stir in remaining flour to make a moderately stiff batter. Spread in greased 13x9x2-inch baking pan. Cover and let rise in warm place till double (45 to 60 minutes). Stir together 1½ cups sugar and the cinnamon. Combine beaten egg yolk and cream; add to sugar mixture, stirring till blended. Add rhubarb. Carefully spoon atop risen dough. Bake at 400° for 20 to 25 minutes. Cut and serve warm. Makes 1 coffee cake.

SWEDISH TEA RING

1 package active dry yeast
¼ cup warm water (110°)
¾ cup milk
⅓ cup sugar
⅓ cup shortening
1 teaspoon salt
4 to 4½ cups all-purpose flour
2 eggs
2 tablespoons butter, melted
Raisin Filling
Confectioners' Icing (see page 26)

Soften active dry yeast in the warm water. Combine milk, sugar, shortening, and salt. Heat till sugar dissolves. Cool to lukewarm. Stir in *2 cups* of the flour; beat well. Add the softened yeast and eggs; beat well. Stir in enough of the remaining flour to make a soft dough. Turn out on a lightly floured surface and knead till smooth and elastic (8 to 10 minutes). Shape into a ball. Place in lightly greased bowl, turning once to grease surface. Cover; let rise in warm place until double (1 to 1½ hours). Punch dough down; turn out on lightly floured surface. Divide in half.

Cover; let rest 10 minutes. Roll each half into 13x9-inch rectangle. Spread *each* with *1 tablespoon* melted butter; spread *each* with *half* of the Raisin Filling. Roll as for jelly roll, beginning at long side; seal edge. Shape each in ring and place, seam side down, on foil-lined baking sheet; seal ends of rings. With scissors, snip ⅔ of the way to center at 1½-inch intervals. Turn each section slightly to one side. Cover and let rise in warm place till double (about 45 minutes). Bake at 350° for 20 to 25 minutes. Drizzle with Confectioners' Icing. Makes 2 coffee cakes.

Raisin Filling: Combine ¾ cup sugar, ¾ cup raisins, and 2 teaspoons ground cinnamon.

CHOCOLATE CHIP COFFEE RING

1¾ cups all-purpose flour
1 package active dry yeast
½ cup milk
¼ cup butter or margarine
3 tablespoons sugar
½ teaspoon salt
1 egg
½ cup semisweet chocolate pieces
Confectioners' Icing (see page 26)

In large mixer bowl combine *1 cup* of the flour and the yeast. Heat together milk, butter or margarine, sugar, and salt just till warm (115-120°), stirring constantly to melt butter. Add to dry mixture in mixer bowl; add egg. Beat at low speed with electric mixer for ½ minute, scraping sides of bowl constantly. Beat 3 minutes at high speed. By hand, stir in remaining flour. Add chocolate pieces; mix well.

Turn into well-greased 4½-cup ring mold. Cover and let rise in warm place till double (45 to 60 minutes). Bake at 400° for 12 to 15 minutes. Remove from pan immediately; drizzle with Confectioners' Icing while still warm. Serve warm or cool. Makes 1 coffee cake.

FRENCH CHOCOLATE COFFEE CAKE

Chocolate-swirled coffee cake pictured on page 6—

In large mixer bowl combine 1½ cups all-purpose flour and 2 packages active dry yeast. Heat ¾ cup sugar, ⅔ cup water, ½ cup butter, ⅓ cup evaporated milk, and ½ teaspoon salt just till warm (115-120°), stirring constantly to melt butter. Add to dry mixture in mixer bowl. Add 4 egg yolks. Beat at low speed with electric mixer for ½ minute, scraping bowl. Beat 3 minutes at high speed. By hand, stir in 2½ cups all-purpose flour to make a moderately soft dough. Place in greased bowl, turning once. Cover; let rise till double (about 2 hours).

Punch down; turn out on floured surface. Cover; let rest 10 minutes. Meanwhile, combine ¾ cup semisweet chocolate pieces, ⅓ cup evaporated milk, 2 tablespoons sugar, and ½ teaspoon ground cinnamon. Stir over low heat till chocolate melts; cool. Roll dough to 18x10-inch rectangle. Spread with chocolate mixture; roll up from long side. Join ends. Place in greased 10-inch tube pan.

Combine ¼ cup all-purpose flour, ¼ cup sugar, and 1 teaspoon ground cinnamon. Cut in ¼ cup butter; stir in ¼ cup semisweet chocolate pieces and ¼ cup chopped nuts. Sprinkle on dough. Let rise till double (about 1¼ hours). Bake at 350° for 45 to 50 minutes. Cool 15 minutes; remove from pan. Makes 1 coffee cake.

STREUSEL COFFEE CAKE

    2½ to 3 cups all-purpose flour
    1 package active dry yeast
    ½ cup milk
    ⅓ cup sugar
    ⅓ cup butter or margarine
    1 egg
    1 tablespoon grated lemon peel
    ½ teaspoon vanilla
      Streusel Topping

In large mixer bowl combine 1¼ *cups* of the flour and the yeast. Heat milk, sugar, butter, and ¾ teaspoon salt just till warm (115-120°), stirring to melt butter. Add to dry mixture in bowl; add egg, lemon peel, and vanilla. Beat at low speed with electric mixer for ½ minute, scraping bowl. Beat 3 minutes at high speed. By hand, stir in enough of the remaining flour to make a

soft dough. Knead on lightly floured surface till smooth (8 to 10 minutes). Shape into a ball. Place in lightly greased bowl, turning once.

Cover; let rise till double (1½ to 2 hours). Punch down; turn out on lightly floured surface. Divide in half. Cover; let rest 10 minutes. Pat each half evenly into a greased 8x1½-inch round baking pan. Sprinkle *half* of the Streusel Topping over each coffee cake. Cover; let rise till double (30 to 45 minutes). Bake at 375° about 20 minutes. Serve warm. Makes 2.

Streusel Topping: Combine ½ cup all-purpose flour, ⅓ cup packed brown sugar, and 1 teaspoon ground cinnamon. Cut in ⅓ cup butter or margarine till crumbly. Add 2 tablespoons finely chopped nuts. Mix well.

BUBBLE WREATH

    3½ to 3¾ cups all-purpose flour
    1 package active dry yeast
    1¼ cups milk
    ¼ cup sugar
    ¼ cup shortening
    1 egg
      Sugar-Fruit Topping
      Melted butter
    ½ cup sugar
    1 teaspoon ground cinnamon

In large mixer bowl combine *2 cups* of the flour and the yeast. Heat milk, ¼ cup sugar, shortening, and 1 teaspoon salt till warm (115-120°), stirring to melt shortening. Add to dry mixture in bowl; add egg. Beat at low speed with electric mixer for ½ minute, scraping bowl. Beat 3 minutes at high speed. Stir in enough remaining flour to make a soft dough. Turn out on lightly floured surface; knead till smooth.

Place in a greased bowl, turning once to grease surface. Cover; let rise till double (about 2 hours). Grease a 10-inch tube pan; spread bottom with Sugar-Fruit Topping. Shape dough into 48 small balls; roll in melted butter, then in mixture of ½ cup sugar and cinnamon. Place in rows in pan. Let rise till double. Bake at 400° for 35 minutes. Loosen; turn out quickly. Makes 1.

Sugar-Fruit Topping: Melt 2 tablespoons butter; add ½ cup packed brown sugar and 2 tablespoons light corn syrup. Spread in pan. Place ½ cup candied cherry halves, cut side up, and ¼ cup sliced almonds on sugar mixture.

As cheery as its name, *Sunburst Coffee Cake* will brighten up any coffee-time occasion. After you cut the sweet dough with a doughnut cutter, create this unusual design and top with jelly and icing.

Use the doughnut 'holes' to form the coffee cake center. Stretch the doughnut shapes with your fingers, and arrange around cake's center.

Spoon your favorite jelly in the center of the outer rings. Drizzle with Confectioners' Icing, and sprinkle yellow sugar crystals in the center.

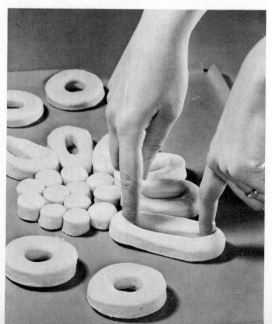

SUNBURST COFFEE CAKE

    2½ to 2¾ cups all-purpose flour
      1 package active dry yeast
      ⅔ cup milk
      ¼ cup sugar
      ¼ cup shortening
      1 egg
      ½ teaspoon grated lemon peel
      ¼ cup currant jelly
        Confectioners' Icing
        (see page 26 – use double recipe)

In large mixer bowl combine *1 cup* of the flour and the yeast. Heat milk, sugar, shortening, and 1 teaspoon salt just till warm (115-120°), stirring to melt shortening. Add to dry mixture; add egg and lemon peel. Beat at low speed with electric mixer for ½ minute, scraping bowl. Beat 3 minutes at high speed. By hand, stir in enough of the remaining flour to make a moderately stiff dough. Knead on a lightly floured surface till smooth and elastic (3 to 5 minutes). Place in greased bowl, turning once. Cover and let rise till double (1 to 1½ hours).

Punch down; turn out on lightly floured surface. Cover and let rest 10 minutes. Roll out to 10x8-inch rectangle. With doughnut cutter, cut into 12 doughnuts. Arrange the doughnut 'holes' in a solid circle on greased baking sheet to form center. Stretch the doughnut rings slightly; arrange around doughnut holes. Let rise again till light (about 45 minutes). Bake at 375° till done, 12 to 15 minutes. Cool on rack. Spoon jelly into center of outer rings. Drizzle with Confectioners' Icing. Sprinkle center with yellow sugar crystals, if desired. Serve warm or cool. Makes 1 coffee cake.

SESAME LOAF

In large mixer bowl combine 1½ cups all-purpose flour and 1 package active dry yeast. Heat ¾ cup milk, ¼ cup sugar, ¼ cup shortening, and 1 teaspoon salt just till warm (115-120°), stirring to melt shortening. Add to dry mixture in bowl; add 1 egg. Beat at low speed with electric mixer for ½ minute, scraping bowl. Beat 3 minutes at high speed. By hand, stir in 1 to 1½ cups all-purpose flour to make a soft dough. Turn out on a lightly floured surface and knead till smooth and elastic (5 to 8 minutes). Shape

into a ball. Place in lightly greased bowl, turning once. Cover; let rise till double (about 1½ hours). Punch dough down; turn out on lightly floured surface. Cover; let rest 10 minutes.

Roll to 15x12-inch rectangle; brush with 1 tablespoon melted butter. Prepare Sesame Seed Filling; reserve ¼ cup and sprinkle remaining filling over dough. Fold dough in thirds to make 15x4-inch rectangle; brush top with about ½ tablespoon melted butter. Cut into 10 equal slices, 1½ inches wide. Cut each slice in half to make twenty 2-inch-long strips. In a greased 9x5x3-inch loaf pan arrange two rows of strips, side by side, with 10 strips in each row. Brush top with about ½ tablespoon melted butter; sprinkle with reserved filling. Cover; let rise till double (about 45 minutes). Bake at 350° for 25 to 30 minutes. Turn out at once. Makes 1.

Sesame Seed Filling: Combine ½ cup sugar, ½ cup chopped walnuts, 2 tablespoons toasted sesame seed, and 1 teaspoon ground cinnamon.

JAM-DOTTED KUCHEN

      2 cups all-purpose flour
      1 package active dry yeast
      ½ cup milk
      6 tablespoons butter or margarine
      ¼ cup sugar
      ½ teaspoon salt
      1 egg
      ⅔ cup jam or preserves
        Streusel-Nut Topping

In large mixer bowl combine *1 cup* of the flour and the yeast. Heat milk, butter, sugar, and salt just till warm (115-120°), stirring to melt butter. Add to mixture in bowl; add egg. Beat at low speed with electric mixer for ½ minute, scraping bowl. Beat 3 minutes at high speed. By hand, stir in enough remaining flour to make a soft dough. Spread in two greased 8x1½-inch round baking pans. Cover; let rise till double (about 1 hour). Carefully make holes at 2-inch intervals in the raised dough. Fill depressions with jam or preserves. Spread *half* of the Streusel-Nut Topping over top of each cake. Bake at 350° for 25 to 30 minutes. Makes 2.

Streusel-Nut Topping: Combine ½ cup all-purpose flour and ⅓ cup packed brown sugar. Cut in ¼ cup butter till crumbly. Add ¼ cup chopped walnuts and 1 teaspoon vanilla; mix.

Creating a ladder loaf

For something a little out of the ordinary, try shaping your next coffee cake ladder-fashion. This shaping technique is pictured below. Roll the dough into a 9-inch square and place it on a greased baking sheet. Spread a filling in a 3-inch strip down the center of the dough. With kitchen shears, snip sides toward the center in strips 3 inches long and 1 inch wide. Then, fold the strips of dough over the filling, alternating from side to side.

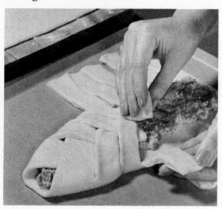

ORANGE-RUM LADDER LOAF

    3½ to 3¾ cups all-purpose flour
    1 package active dry yeast
    1 cup milk
    ⅓ cup sugar
    ¼ cup butter or margarine
    1 teaspoon salt
    1 egg
      Orange-Rum Filling
      Confectioners' Icing (see page 26)

In large mixer bowl combine *2 cups* of the flour and the yeast. Heat milk, sugar, butter, and salt just till warm (115-120°), stirring to melt butter. Add to dry mixture; add egg. Beat at low speed with electric mixer for ½ minute, scraping bowl. Beat 3 minutes at high speed. By hand, stir in enough of the remaining flour to make a moderately stiff dough. Knead on a lightly floured surface till smooth (5 to 8 minutes). Shape into a ball. Place in lightly greased bowl, turning once. Cover; let rise till double (1 to 1¼ hours). Punch dough down; divide in half. Cover; let rest 10 minutes.

Roll each half to a 9-inch square. Place on greased baking sheets. Spread Orange-Rum Filling in a 3-inch strip down center of each square of dough. With kitchen shears, snip sides toward center in strips 3 inches long and 1 inch wide. Fold strips over filling, alternating from side to side. Cover; let rise in warm place till double (30 to 45 minutes). Bake at 375° about 15 minutes. Cool slightly; drizzle with Confectioners' Icing. Makes 2 coffee cakes.

Orange-Rum Filling: Mix ½ cup orange marmalade, ½ cup flaked coconut, 2 tablespoons brown sugar, and ½ teaspoon rum flavoring.

CHEESECAKE BREAD RING

Coffee bread made in a ring mold is shown on page 4—

    1 13¾-ounce package hot roll mix
    ¼ cup sugar
    3 eggs
    ½ cup dairy sour cream
    6 tablespoons butter, melted
    1 8-ounce package cream cheese,
      softened
    ½ cup sugar
    1 teaspoon vanilla

Soften yeast from hot roll mix in ¼ cup *warm* water (110°). Combine roll mix and ¼ cup sugar. Stir in yeast, *1 egg,* sour cream, and butter; mix well. Place dough in lightly greased bowl, turning once. Cover; chill 2 to 3 hours. Turn dough out onto lightly floured surface. Roll dough into an 18-inch circle. Gently fit into a 6½-cup ring mold, allowing dough to cover center and some to hang over edges.

Beat cream cheese, ½ cup sugar, and vanilla till smooth. Add remaining 2 eggs, one at a time, beating well after each. Pour into mold. Bring dough from sides over top of filling; seal to dough at rim of center hole. Cut an 'X' in the dough covering the hole; fold the four triangles back over top of ring, sealing to outer edges. Let rise till almost double (1 to 1½ hours). Bake at 350° for 35 to 40 minutes. Cool in pan 10 minutes; turn out on rack. Sprinkle with powdered sugar, if desired. Makes 1 coffee cake.

APRICOT-TOPPED COFFEE BREAD

This daisy coffee cake is shown on page 9 —

    3 to 3½ cups all-purpose flour
    1 package active dry yeast
    ¾ cup milk
    ¼ cup butter or margarine
    1 tablespoon sugar
    2 tablespoons honey
    2 eggs
    ½ cup apricot preserves
    2 tablespoons chopped walnuts
       Confectioners' Icing (see page 26)

In large mixer bowl combine *1½ cups* of the flour and the yeast. Heat milk, butter, sugar, *1 tablespoon* of the honey, and 1 teaspoon salt just till warm (115-120°), stirring to melt butter. Add to dry mixture in bowl; add eggs. Beat at low speed with electric mixer for ½ minute, scraping bowl. Beat 3 minutes at high speed. Stir in enough remaining flour to make a moderately stiff dough. Knead on a floured surface till smooth. Place in greased bowl, turning once. Cover; let rise till double (about 1¼ hours). Punch down; cover and let rest 10 minutes.

Roll dough to 14-inch circle. Place a glass tumbler in center. Cut dough in quarters up to the glass. Cut each section into 5 strips in the same manner, making 20 strips. Twist two strips together; continue around circle, making 10 twists. Remove glass. Remove and reserve one twist; coil the reserved twist in center. Coil remaining twists toward center to form daisy design. Let rise till double (about 45 minutes). Bake at 375° for 20 to 25 minutes. Combine preserves, nuts, and remaining 1 tablespoon honey; spoon atop. Glaze with Icing. Makes 1.

PRUNE AND CHEESE CAKE

In large mixer bowl combine 1 cup all-purpose flour and 1 package active dry yeast. Heat ¾ cup milk, 2 tablespoons sugar, 2 tablespoons shortening, and ½ teaspoon salt till warm (115-120°), stirring to melt shortening. Add to dry mixture; add 1 egg. Beat at low speed with mixer for ½ minute, scraping bowl. Beat 3 minutes at high speed. By hand, stir in 1⅓ cups all-purpose flour. Place in greased bowl; turn once. Cover and chill well, 2 to 3 hours.

Pat dough evenly into greased 15½x10½x1-inch baking pan, forming ridge around edges. Spread with one 12-ounce can prune filling. Let rise in warm place till almost double (about 45 minutes). Bake at 375° about 15 minutes. Combine one 12-ounce carton cream-style cottage cheese (1½ cups), 2 tablespoons sugar, 1 tablespoon all-purpose flour, ½ teaspoon grated lemon peel, and ¼ teaspoon ground cinnamon. Beat in 1 egg. Spread atop filling. Combine ¼ cup graham cracker crumbs and 2 teaspoons sugar; sprinkle atop. Bake 10 minutes. Makes 1.

Shape *Apricot-Topped Coffee Bread* by twisting pairs of dough strips together around a glass placed in center. Pinch ends. Remove glass.

Remove and reserve one twist. Coil reserved twist in center of dough to form daisy center. Coil remaining twists toward center.

Savory Sweet Rolls

BASIC SWEET ROLL DOUGH

In large mixer bowl combine 2 cups all-purpose flour and 1 package active dry yeast. Heat 1 cup milk, ¼ cup sugar, ¼ cup shortening, and 1 teaspoon salt till warm (115-120°), stirring to melt shortening. Add to dry mixture; add 2 eggs. Beat at low speed with electric mixer for ½ minute, scraping bowl. Beat 3 minutes at high speed. By hand, stir in 1½ to 2 cups all-purpose flour to make a moderately stiff dough. Knead on lightly floured surface till smooth (8 to 10 minutes). Shape into a ball. Place in greased bowl, turning once. Cover; let rise till double (45 to 60 minutes). Punch down; divide in half. Cover; let rest 10 minutes.

Rolling dough for sweet rolls

Roll a portion of dough into a rectangle, following size given in the recipe. Spread filling evenly over dough to within about ½ inch of edges (if filling is very soft, spread only to 1 inch of edges). Roll dough up, starting with long side as for jelly roll, and seal seam securely. Spreading a little water at the seam helps to make a tighter seal. For larger but fewer rolls, try rolling the dough starting at the short side.

CINNAMON ROLLS

Old-time favorite pictured on the cover —

  Basic Sweet Roll Dough
  ¼ **cup butter or margarine, melted**
  ½ **cup sugar**
  2 **teaspoons ground cinnamon**
  ¾ **cup raisins (optional)**
  Confectioners' Icing (see page 26)

Roll each half of Basic Sweet Roll Dough into a 12x8-inch rectangle. Brush *each* with *half* the melted butter. Combine sugar and cinnamon; sprinkle over dough. Sprinkle with raisins, if desired. Roll up each piece, starting with long side; seal seams. Slice each into 12 rolls. Place rolls, cut side down, in two greased 9x1½-inch round baking pans. Cover and let rise till double (about 35 minutes). Bake at 375° for 18 to 20 minutes. Drizzle Icing over warm rolls. Makes 24.

CARAMEL-PECAN ROLLS

  Basic Sweet Roll Dough
  3 **tablespoons butter, melted**
  ½ **cup granulated sugar**
  1 **teaspoon ground cinnamon**
  ⅔ **cup packed brown sugar**
  ¼ **cup butter or margarine**
  2 **tablespoons light corn syrup**
  ½ **cup chopped pecans**

Roll each half of Basic Sweet Roll Dough into a 12x8-inch rectangle. Brush *each* with *half* the melted butter. Combine granulated sugar and cinnamon; sprinkle over dough. Roll up each piece of dough, starting with long side; seal seams. Slice each roll into 12 pieces. In saucepan combine brown sugar, ¼ cup butter, and corn syrup. Cook and stir just till butter melts and mixture is blended. Distribute mixture evenly in two 9x1½-inch round baking pans. Top with pecans. Place rolls, cut side down, in prepared baking pans. Cover; let rise till double (about 30 minutes). Bake at 375° for 18 to 20 minutes. Cool about 30 seconds; invert on rack and remove pans. Makes 24.

CREAMY CINNAMON ROLLS

Roll each half of Basic Sweet Roll Dough to a 12x8-inch rectangle. Brush *each* with 1½ tablespoons melted butter. Combine ⅔ cup packed brown sugar, ½ cup chopped walnuts, and 2 teaspoons ground cinnamon; sprinkle atop. Roll up from long side; seal seams. Slice each into 12 rolls. Place in two greased 9x1½-inch round baking pans. Cover; let rise till double (about 30 minutes). Drizzle ¾ cup whipping cream over rolls. Bake at 375° for 18 to 20 minutes. Cool slightly; remove. Drizzle with Confectioners' Icing *(see page 26)*. Makes 24.

GLAZED ORANGE ROLLS

  4¼ to 4½ cups all-purpose flour
  1 package active dry yeast
  1 cup milk
  ½ cup granulated sugar
  3 tablespoons butter or margarine
  3 eggs
  6 tablespoons butter, softened
  ½ cup granulated sugar
  1½ teaspoons shredded orange peel
  1½ cups sifted powdered sugar
  2 to 3 tablespoons orange juice

In large mixer bowl combine *2 cups* of the flour and the yeast. Heat milk, ½ cup sugar, 3 tablespoons butter, and ½ teaspoon salt till warm (115-120°), stirring to melt butter. Add to dry mixture; add eggs. Beat at low speed with mixer for ½ minute, scraping bowl. Beat 3 minutes at high speed. Stir in enough remaining flour to make a moderately soft dough. Knead on floured surface till smooth (3 to 5 minutes). Place in greased bowl; turn once. Cover; let rise till double (1 to 1½ hours). Punch down; divide in half. Cover; let rest 10 minutes.

  Roll each half to 12x8-inch rectangle. Combine 6 tablespoons butter, ½ cup sugar, and peel; spread over dough. Roll up, starting with long side; seal seams. Slice each into 12 rolls. Place, cut side down, in greased 2½-inch muffin pans. (Or, use two 9x1½-inch round baking pans for softer rolls.) Cover; let rise till double (about 1½ hours). Bake at 375° for 15 to 20 minutes. Remove from pan immediately. Combine powdered sugar and orange juice for glaze consistency. Drizzle over warm rolls. Makes 24.

Set a bowl of sweet, softened butter next to a plate of fragrant, warm-from-the-oven *Glazed Orange Rolls,* and watch them disappear.

PEANUT BUTTER-JELLY TWISTS

  2¼ cups all-purpose flour
  1 package active dry yeast
  ½ cup milk
  ¼ cup sugar
  3 tablespoons butter or margarine
  1 egg
  ⅓ cup peanut butter
  ⅓ cup red jam or preserves
  1 tablespoon butter, melted

In large mixer bowl combine *1 cup* of the flour and the yeast. Heat milk, sugar, butter, and 1 teaspoon salt till warm (115-120°), stirring to melt butter. Add to dry mixture; add egg. Beat at low speed with mixer for ½ minute, scraping bowl. Beat 3 minutes at high speed. Stir in remaining flour; beat well. Cover; let rest ½ hour.

Roll dough to 16x10-inch rectangle. Spread peanut butter over lengthwise half; spread jam on top. Fold to make 16x5-inch rectangle; seal edges. Cut crosswise into 1-inch strips. Loosely twist each; arrange in greased 11x7½x1½-inch baking dish. Brush with melted butter. Cover; let rise till double (about 1¼ hours). Bake at 375° for 15 to 20 minutes. Makes 16.

FRENCH LEMON SPIRALS

In large mixer bowl combine 1 cup all-purpose flour and 1 package active dry yeast. Heat ½ cup milk, 6 tablespoons butter or margarine, ¼ cup sugar, and ¼ teaspoon salt till warm (115-120°), stirring to melt butter. Add to dry mixture; add 2 eggs and 2 teaspoons grated lemon peel. Beat at low speed with electric mixer for ½ minute, scraping bowl. Beat 3 minutes at high speed. By hand, stir in 1¼ to 1½ cups all-purpose flour to make a moderately stiff dough.

Cover; chill 2 to 3 hours. On lightly floured surface, roll *half* the dough to 12x7-inch rectangle. Spread with 1 tablespoon softened butter or margarine. Combine ¼ cup sugar and 1 teaspoon grated lemon peel; sprinkle *half* over the rectangle. Roll up jelly-roll fashion, starting with long side; cut into 12 slices. Repeat shaping with remaining dough, using another 1 tablespoon softened butter and remaining sugar mixture. Place slices, cut side down, on greased baking sheet. Cover; let rise 30 to 35 minutes. Bake at 375° for 12 to 15 minutes. Makes 24.

CINNAMON CRISPS

  3½ cups all-purpose flour
  1 package active dry yeast
  1¼ cups milk
  ¼ cup granulated sugar
  ¼ cup shortening
  1 teaspoon salt
  1 egg
  ¼ cup butter or margarine, melted
  ½ cup packed brown sugar
  ½ cup granulated sugar
  ½ teaspoon ground cinnamon
  ¼ cup butter or margarine, melted
  • • •
  1 cup granulated sugar
  ½ cup chopped pecans
  1 teaspoon ground cinnamon

In large mixer bowl combine *2 cups* of the flour and the yeast. In saucepan heat milk, ¼ cup granulated sugar, shortening, and salt just till warm (115-120°), stirring constantly to melt shortening. Add to dry ingredients in mixer bowl; add egg. Beat at low speed with electric mixer for ½ minute, scraping sides of bowl constantly. Beat 3 minutes at high speed. By hand, stir in enough of the remaining flour to make a moderately soft dough. Shape into a ball. Place dough in a lightly greased bowl, turning once to grease surface. Cover and let rise in a warm place until double (1½ to 2 hours). Punch down; turn out on lightly floured surface. Divide dough in half. Cover; let rest 10 minutes.

Roll out one portion of dough at a time to a 12-inch square. Combine ¼ cup melted butter, brown sugar, ½ cup granulated sugar, and ½ teaspoon ground cinnamon. Spread *half* of mixture over dough. Roll up lengthwise jelly-roll fashion; pinch to seal edges. Cut into 12 rolls. Place on greased baking sheets at least 3 inches apart. Flatten each to about 3 inches in diameter. Repeat with remaining dough and sugar mixture. Let rise in warm place (about 30 minutes).

Cover with waxed paper. Roll over tops with rolling pin to flatten to ⅛-inch thickness. Carefully remove paper. Brush tops of rolls with remaining melted butter. Combine remaining 1 cup granulated sugar, pecans, and 1 teaspoon ground cinnamon. Sprinkle over rolls. Cover with waxed paper; roll flat again. Remove paper. Bake at 400° for 10 to 12 minutes. Remove immediately from baking sheets. Makes 24.

You won't have to buy *Cinnamon Crisps* at a bakery once you've discovered that you can prepare them in your own kitchen. The luscious pastry spirals are pressed full of cinnamon, sugar, and pecans.

Spread the dough with a mixture of butter, brown sugar, granulated sugar, and cinnamon. Roll up lengthwise jelly-roll fashion; seal the edges.

Cut roll into 12 even pieces. Place on greased baking sheet at least 3 inches apart. Flatten each to about 3 inches in diameter. Allow to rise 30 minutes.

Cover with waxed paper. Flatten with rolling pin to about ⅛-inch thickness. Remove paper. Top with butter, sugar, nuts, and cinnamon. Cover; roll flat.

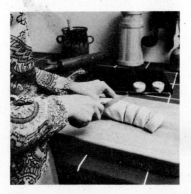

Cutting rolls with a thread

Cutting a filled sweet roll dough, such as cinnamon roll dough, is especially easy when it's done with thread. Use ordinary sewing weight or heavy-duty white thread. Cut off a long enough piece of thread so you can work comfortably. Place thread under the rolled dough where you want to make the cut, and pull up around sides. Then, crisscross thread across top of roll, and pull quickly as though tieing a knot.

A sharp knife also can be used to cut roll dough. However, with a knife it's much more difficult to keep from squashing the rolls.

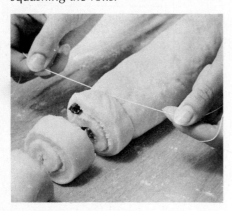

CHOCOLATE-ORANGE ROLLS

Combine 1½ cups all-purpose flour and 1 package active dry yeast. In saucepan heat ½ cup milk, ¼ cup sugar, 2 tablespoons butter or margarine, and ½ teaspoon salt till warm (115-120°), stirring to melt butter. Add to dry mixture; add 2 eggs. Beat at low speed with electric mixer for ½ minute, scraping bowl. Beat 3 minutes at high speed. By hand, stir in ¾ to 1 cup all-purpose flour to make a moderately soft dough.

Turn out onto lightly floured surface; knead till smooth and elastic (4 to 5 minutes). Place in lightly greased bowl; turn once. Cover; let rise in warm place till double (about 1 hour). Punch down; cover and let rest 10 minutes. Roll dough to 15x10-inch rectangle. Spread with 2 tablespoons softened butter. Combine ¼ cup sugar and 1 tablespoon shredded orange peel. Sprinkle dough with sugar mixture, then with ½ cup semisweet chocolate pieces. Roll up jelly-roll fashion, starting with long side. Cut roll into 18 slices; place 9 slices, cut side down, in each of two greased 9x9x2-inch baking pans. Let dough rise in warm place till nearly double (25 to 30 minutes). Bake at 375° for 12 to 15 minutes. Remove from pans and cool. Makes 18.

LEMON PUFF PILLOW BUNS

3¼ cups all-purpose flour
1 package active dry yeast
¾ cup milk
6 tablespoons butter or margarine
¼ cup sugar
1 teaspoon salt
2 eggs
1 teaspoon grated lemon peel
4 3-ounce packages cream cheese, softened
3 tablespoons sugar
1 egg yolk
1 teaspoon vanilla
1 beaten egg white

In large mixer bowl combine *1½ cups* of the flour and the yeast. In saucepan heat milk, butter, ¼ cup sugar, and salt just till warm (115-120°), stirring constantly to melt butter. Add to dry mixture in mixer bowl; add 2 eggs and lemon peel. Beat at low speed with electric mixer for ½ minute, scraping sides of bowl constantly. Beat 3 minutes at high speed. By hand, stir in the remaining flour. Cover bowl lightly; refrigerate dough at least 4 hours or overnight.

When ready to shape, blend together cream cheese, 3 tablespoons sugar, egg yolk, and vanilla. Divide dough in fourths. On generously floured surface, roll each portion into a 12x8-inch rectangle. (Keep remaining dough refrigerated.) With floured knife cut in six 4-inch squares. Place about 1 tablespoon cream cheese mixture in the center of each; bring opposite corners to the center and pinch to seal. Place 2 inches apart on a greased baking sheet. Brush with beaten egg white. Let rise, *uncovered*, in warm place till half again as large, not double (20 to 30 minutes). Bake at 400° till done, about 10 minutes. Serve hot. Makes 24.

DOUGHNUTS

  3 to 3½ cups all-purpose flour
  2 packages active dry yeast
  ¾ cup milk
  ⅓ cup sugar
  ¼ cup shortening
  1 teaspoon salt
  2 eggs
  Glaze (optional)

In large mixer bowl combine *1½ cups* of the flour and the yeast. In saucepan heat together milk, sugar, shortening, and salt just till warm (115-120°), stirring constantly to melt shortening. Add to dry mixture in mixer bowl; add eggs. Beat at low speed with electric mixer for ½ minute, scraping sides of bowl constantly. Beat 3 minutes at high speed. By hand, stir in enough of the remaining flour to make a moderately soft dough. Turn out onto a lightly floured surface and knead till smooth and elastic (5 to 8 minutes). Shape into a ball. Place in lightly greased bowl, turning once to grease surface.

Cover and let rise in warm place till double (45 to 60 minutes). Punch dough down; turn out onto a lightly floured surface. Divide in half. Roll out dough to ½-inch thickness. Cut with floured doughnut cutter (has hole in center) into doughnuts. Cover and let rise in warm place till very light (about 30 to 45 minutes). Fry in deep hot fat (375°) till golden, about 1 minute on each side. Drain on paper toweling. If desired, roll warm doughnuts in sugar or frost with Glaze. Makes 18 to 20.

Glaze: Combine 2 cups sifted powdered sugar, ¼ cup milk, and 1 teaspoon vanilla.

Chocolate Doughnuts: Prepare Doughnuts as above, *except* heat two 1-ounce squares semisweet chocolate with milk, sugar, shortening, and salt. Cover and let dough rise 1 to 1½ hours the first time. Cut with floured doughnut cutter. Let rise. Fry in deep hot fat (365°) about 45 seconds on each side. Roll the doughnuts in sugar, or frost them with Chocolate Glaze.

Chocolate Glaze: In saucepan, melt together two 1-ounce squares semisweet chocolate and 2 tablespoons butter over low heat. Add 2 cups sifted powdered sugar and 1 teaspoon vanilla. Stir in ¼ cup boiling water till mixture is smooth. Dip doughnuts in glaze, then in ½ cup finely chopped walnuts. Makes 18 to 20.

BISMARCKS

Prepare Doughnuts, cutting with a round 2½-inch floured cookie cutter (no hole in center). Let rise and fry as directed. Drain. With a sharp knife cut a wide slit in the side of each cooked doughnut. Insert 2 teaspoons jam or jelly into each. *Or,* make a narrow slit in the side of each doughnut and use a cake decorating tube with narrow point or a spoon to insert jam or jelly. Roll bismarcks in granulated or powdered sugar. Makes 18 to 20 bismarcks.

Cream-Filled Bismarcks: Prepare Doughnuts, cutting with a round 2½-inch floured cookie cutter (no hole in center). With sharp knife cut cooked doughnuts in half crosswise. In mixer bowl cream together ¼ cup butter or margarine, ¼ cup shortening, ½ cup granulated sugar, and ½ teaspoon vanilla. Gradually beat in ½ cup milk (room temperature) till mixture is fluffy. Spoon about 1 tablespoon filling onto bottom halves of doughnuts. Dip top halves in powdered sugar; place on bottom halves of doughnuts.

FRENCH DOUGHNUTS

  3 cups all-purpose flour
  1 package active dry yeast
  ½ teaspoon ground nutmeg
  1 cup milk
  ¼ cup sugar
  ¼ cup cooking oil
  1 egg
  Powdered sugar

In large mixer bowl combine *1½ cups* of the flour, yeast, and nutmeg. In saucepan heat milk, sugar, oil, and ¾ teaspoon salt just till warm (115-120°). Add to dry mixture in bowl; add egg. Beat at low speed with electric mixer for ½ minute, scraping bowl. Beat 3 minutes at high speed. By hand, stir in enough remaining flour to make a soft dough. Place in greased bowl; turn once. Cover and chill.

Turn dough out on well floured surface; form into ball. Cover; let rest 10 minutes. Roll to 18x12-inch rectangle. Cut in 3x2-inch rectangles. Cover; let rise (30 minutes)—dough will not be doubled. Fry in deep hot fat (375°), turning once, till golden, about 1 minute. Drain. Sprinkle with powdered sugar. Makes 36.

DANISH PASTRY

1 cup butter or margarine
⅓ cup all-purpose flour
3¾ to 4 cups all-purpose flour
2 packages active dry yeast
1¼ cups milk
¼ cup sugar
1 teaspoon salt
1 egg
½ teaspoon lemon extract
½ teaspoon almond extract
Confectioners' Icing (see page 26)

Cream butter or margarine with ⅓ cup flour. Pat or roll butter mixture between 2 sheets of waxed paper to 12x6-inch rectangle. *Chill thoroughly.* In large mixer bowl combine *1½ cups* of the remaining flour and the yeast. In saucepan heat milk, sugar, and salt just till warm (115-120°). Add to dry mixture in mixer bowl; add egg and extracts. Beat at low speed with electric mixer for ½ minute, scraping sides of bowl constantly. Beat 3 minutes at high speed.

By hand, stir in enough of the remaining flour to make a moderately soft dough. Knead on a lightly floured surface till smooth and elastic (about 5 minutes). Cover; let rest 10 minutes. On lightly floured surface, roll dough to 14-inch square. Place the *chilled* butter on half the dough. Fold over other half, sealing edges well with heel of hand. Roll dough to 20x12-inch rectangle. Fold in thirds (you now have three layers). Roll again to a 20x12-inch rectangle. If butter softens, chill after each rolling. Repeat rolling and folding two more times. Chill 30 minutes. Shape into *Almond Fans* and *Baby Bunting Rolls*. Place on *ungreased* baking sheet. Let rise till almost double (45 to 60 minutes). Bake at 450° about 8 minutes. Brush with Confectioners' Icing. Serve warm. Makes 36.

Almond Fans: Cream together ¼ cup butter and ¼ cup sugar. Add ¼ cup finely chopped blanched almonds; mix well. Roll one-third of dough to 12x8-inch rectangle. Cut in 4x2-inch rectangles; place 1 level teaspoon of the almond filling along center of each. Fold lengthwise. Seal edges; curve rolls slightly. Snip side opposite sealed edge at 1-inch intervals.

Baby Bunting Rolls: In mixer bowl combine ½ cup cooked, dried pitted prunes, ¼ cup sugar, 1 tablespoon all-purpose flour, dash salt, and 1 tablespoon lemon juice. Roll remaining two-thirds of dough into 18x12-inch rectangle; cut in 3-inch squares. Place 1 level teaspoon of the prune filling in center of each square. Fold opposite corners of pastry to center; overlap edges and seal well so they will not unfold.

Prepare chilled butter layer and *Danish Pastry* dough. Peel waxed paper from one side of butter; pat butter on half of dough. Remove paper.

Fold dough over butter; roll in a rectangle. Fold in thirds. Seal edges. Repeat folding and rolling 2 more times. If butter softens, chill dough.

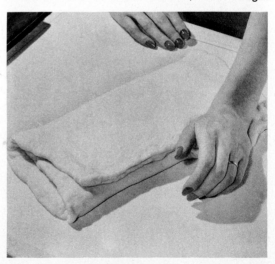

Lighten up the coffee klatch with flaky and rich *Danish Pastry* served on a silver platter. To give the pastry its flaky texture, layer chilled butter with the sweetened yeast dough before baking.

Make *Almond Fans* with one-third of the dough. Seal almond filling in each rectangle. Curve slightly. Snip unsealed edge at 1-inch intervals.

Use remaining two-thirds dough to make *Baby Bunting Rolls.* Fold opposite corners over filling to center. Overlap edges; seal.

SPECIALTY YEAST BREADS

Do you feel in the mood for baking a special type of yeast bread? Then look in this section for an assortment of natural, sourdough, foreign, and holiday bread recipes. Natural breads are made with whole wheat and other flours.

Today, with the emphasis on good nutrition, natural breads not only are good for you, they also taste good and have an interesting flavor and texture. Sourdough breads are also special in that a starter is used as part of the leavening. This starter imparts a tangy flavor that is unique to sourdough breads.

To round out your holiday feast or a dinner planned around a foreign theme, try one of the holiday- or foreign-bread recipes. Also, remember the gift-giving possibilities of a home-baked holiday bread.

For your next French-inspired meal, serve one of these special types of breads — *French Bread, Croissants, or Raisin Brioche Ring.* (See index for page numbers.)

Natural and Sourdough Breads

SUNFLOWER SEED BREAD

    3½ to 4 cups unbleached white flour
    1 package active dry yeast
    ½ cup milk
    3 tablespoons sugar
    2 tablespoons butter or margarine
    1 egg
    1 tablespoon grated orange peel
    ½ cup orange juice
    ⅔ cup shelled sunflower seeds

In large mixer bowl combine 1½ cups of the flour and the yeast. Heat milk, sugar, butter, and 1½ teaspoons salt till warm (115-120°), stirring constantly to melt butter. Add to dry mixture in mixer bowl; add egg, peel, and juice. Beat at low speed with electric mixer for ½ minute, scraping bowl. Beat 3 minutes at high speed. By hand, stir in sunflower seeds and enough remaining flour to make a stiff dough.

Knead on lightly floured surface till smooth (5 to 8 minutes). Place in greased bowl, turning once. Cover; let rise in warm place till double (about 1½ hours). Punch down. Cover; let rest 10 minutes. Shape into loaf and place in greased 8½x4½x2½-inch loaf pan. Cover; let rise till double (45 to 60 minutes). Brush top with melted butter, if desired. Bake at 375° about 40 minutes. Remove from pan and cool. Makes 1 loaf.

PEASANT BREAD

    3 to 3¼ cups unbleached white flour
    2 packages active dry yeast
    1¾ cups warm water (110°)
    ¼ cup dark molasses
    2 tablespoons cooking oil
    2 teaspoons salt
    1½ cups rye flour
    ½ cup whole bran cereal
    ⅓ cup yellow cornmeal
    1 tablespoon caraway seed

In large mixer bowl combine 2 cups of the unbleached white flour and the yeast. Combine water, molasses, oil, and salt. Add to dry mixture in mixer bowl. Beat at low speed with electric mixer for ½ minute, scraping sides of bowl constantly. Beat 3 minutes at high speed. By hand, stir in rye flour, bran cereal, cornmeal, caraway seed, and enough of the remaining white flour to make a moderately stiff dough.

Turn out on lightly floured surface and knead till smooth and elastic (8 to 10 minutes). Shape in ball. Place in lightly greased bowl, turning once to grease surface. Cover; let rise in warm place till double (1 to 1¼ hours). Punch down; turn out on lightly floured surface. Divide in half. Cover; let rest 10 minutes. Shape into two loaves without rolling, and place loaves in two greased 8½x4½x2½-inch loaf pans. Cover and let rise in warm place till double (30 to 45 minutes). Bake at 375° for 35 to 40 minutes. Remove from pan and cool. Makes 2 loaves.

RYE PRETZELS

    1 package active dry yeast
    1 tablespoon malted milk powder
    1 tablespoon caraway seed
    1 tablespoon molasses
    4½ cups rye flour
    Coarse salt

Soften yeast in 1½ cups *warm* water (110°). Add malted milk powder, caraway seed, molasses, and 1 teaspoon salt. Stir in rye flour. Knead on floured surface till smooth (about 5 minutes). Cut into 12 portions; roll each to a rope 15 inches long. Shape into pretzels; place on greased baking sheet. Moisten lightly with water; sprinkle with coarse salt. Bake at 425° till browned and crisp, 15 to 20 minutes. Remove from pan and cool. Makes 12 pretzels.

A nourishing assortment of breads

Full-flavored specialty flours and seeds are → blended to make *Peasant Bread* (left), *Sunflower Seed Bread* (right), and *Rye Pretzels*. Enjoy the old-time goodness of these hearty breads.

...AT BREAD

...ed bread is shown on cover—

... whole wheat flour
...ctive dry yeast
... cups milk
⅓ cup packed brown sugar
2 tablespoons shortening
2 teaspoons salt

In large mixer bowl combine *2 cups* of the flour and the yeast. In saucepan heat milk, brown sugar, shortening, and salt just till warm (115-120°), stirring constantly to melt shortening. Add to dry mixture in mixer bowl. Beat at low speed with electric mixer for ½ minute, scraping sides of bowl constantly. Beat 3 minutes at high speed. By hand, stir in enough of the remaining flour to make a moderately stiff dough.

Turn out onto lightly floured surface and knead till smooth and elastic (4 to 5 minutes). Shape in a ball. Place in lightly greased bowl, turning once to grease surface. Cover; let rise in warm place until double (1 to 1½ hours). Punch dough down; turn out on lightly floured surface. Cover; let rest 10 minutes.

Shape in a loaf; place in greased 8½x4½x2½-inch loaf pan. Cover and let rise in warm place till double (about 30 minutes). Bake at 375° for 35 to 40 minutes. Remove from pan and cool on wire rack. Makes 1 loaf.

SEVEN-GRAIN CEREAL BREAD

½ cup seven-grain cereal
6 tablespoons butter or margarine
¼ cup honey
2 teaspoons salt
• • •
5 to 5¼ cups unbleached white flour
2 packages active dry yeast
2 eggs
1 egg yolk
1 tablespoon poppy or sesame seed
   (optional)

In small saucepan combine 7-grain cereal and 1 cup water. Cook, covered, 20 minutes. Stir in 1 cup water, butter, honey, and salt; cool to lukewarm. In large mixer bowl combine *2 cups* of the flour and the yeast. Add cereal mixture and the 2 eggs. Beat at low speed with electric mixer for ½ minute, scraping sides of bowl constantly. Beat 3 minutes at high speed. By hand, stir in enough of the remaining unbleached white flour to make a soft dough. Turn out onto lightly floured surface and knead till smooth and elastic (5 to 8 minutes). Shape dough in a ball.

Place dough in lightly greased bowl, turning once to grease surface. Cover and let rise in warm place until double (1 to 1¼ hours). Punch dough down; turn out on lightly floured surface. Divide in half. Cover; let rest 10 minutes. Shape into two loaves and place in two greased 8½x4½x2½-inch loaf pans.

Cover; let rise in warm place till double (45 to 60 minutes). Combine egg yolk with 1 tablespoon water; brush on tops of loaves. Sprinkle with poppy or sesame seed, if desired. Bake at 375° for 30 to 35 minutes. Remove from pans and cool on wire rack. Makes 2 loaves.

PUMPKIN SEED-WHEAT BREAD

4¾ to 5¼ cups whole wheat flour
2 packages active dry yeast
2⅓ cups milk
½ cup honey
2 tablespoons cooking oil
1 tablespoon salt
1 cup pumpkin seeds, coarsely chopped

In large mixer bowl combine *2 cups* of the flour and the yeast. In saucepan heat milk, honey, oil, and salt just till warm (115-120°). Add to dry mixture in mixer bowl. Beat at low speed with electric mixer for ½ minute, scraping sides of bowl constantly. Beat 3 minutes at high speed. By hand, stir in pumpkin seeds and enough of the remaining flour to make a soft dough.

Turn out onto lightly floured surface and knead till smooth and elastic (about 10 minutes). Shape in a ball. Place in lightly greased bowl, turning once to grease surface. Cover; let rise in warm place till double (about 2 hours). Punch dough down; turn out on lightly floured surface. Divide in half.

Cover; let rest 10 minutes. Shape into two loaves and place in two greased 8½x4½x2½-inch loaf pans. Cover and let rise till double (about 1¼ hours). Bake at 375° about 45 minutes. If crust browns too quickly, cover loosely with foil the last 15 minutes. Remove bread from pans and cool on wire rack. Makes 2 loaves.

BROWN RICE BREAD

　2½ to 3 cups unbleached white flour
　　1 package active dry yeast
　　1 cup milk
　　2 tablespoons honey
　　2 tablespoons cooking oil
　　2 teaspoons salt
　　1 egg
　　½ cup brown rice flour

In large mixer bowl combine *1½ cups* of the un-bleached white flour and the yeast. In saucepan heat milk, honey, oil, and salt just till warm (115-120°). Add to dry mixture in mixer bowl; add egg. Beat at low speed with electric mixer for ½ minute, scraping sides of bowl constantly. Beat 3 minutes at high speed.

By hand, stir in brown rice flour and enough of the remaining unbleached white flour to make a soft dough. Turn dough out onto lightly floured surface and knead till smooth and elastic (8 to 10 minutes). Shape in a ball. Place ball of dough in lightly greased bowl, turning once to grease surface. Cover and let rise in warm place until double (1 to 1½ hours).

Punch dough down; turn out on lightly floured surface. Cover; let rest 10 minutes. Shape into a loaf and place in greased 8½x4½x 2½-inch loaf pan. Cover and let rise in warm place until double (about 45 minutes). Bake at 375° about 30 minutes. Remove bread from pan and cool on wire rack. Makes 1 loaf.

HONEY-OATMEAL BREAD

　4½ to 4¾ cups whole wheat flour
　　3 packages active dry yeast
　　2 cups milk
　　⅓ cup honey
　　¼ cup cooking oil
　　1 tablespoon salt
　　½ cup Scotch oats

In large mixer bowl combine *2 cups* of the flour and the yeast. In saucepan heat milk, honey, oil, and salt just till warm (115-120°). Add to dry mixture in mixer bowl. Beat at low speed with electric mixer for ½ minute, scraping sides of bowl constantly. Beat 3 minutes at high speed. By hand, stir in oats and enough of the remaining flour to make a stiff dough. Turn out onto

lightly floured surface and knead till smooth and elastic (8 to 10 minutes). Shape in a ball. Place in lightly greased bowl, turning once to grease surface. Cover; let rise in warm place until double (about 45 minutes).

Punch dough down; turn out on lightly floured surface. Divide in half. Cover; let rest 10 minutes. Shape into two loaves; place in two greased 8½x4½x2½-inch loaf pans. Cover; let rise in warm place till double (about 30 minutes). Bake at 375° for 35 to 40 minutes. Remove from pans; cool on wire racks. Makes 2.

CRACKED WHEAT BREAD

　4 to 4¼ cups unbleached white flour
　　1 cup cracked wheat
　　2 packages active dry yeast
　1½ cups water
　　½ cup milk
　　3 tablespoons sugar
　　3 tablespoons butter or margarine
　　1 tablespoon salt
　　1 cup whole wheat flour

In large mixer bowl combine *2 cups* of the un-bleached white flour, cracked wheat, and active dry yeast. In saucepan heat water, milk, sugar, butter or margarine, and salt just till warm (115-120°), stirring constantly to melt butter. Add to dry mixture in mixer bowl.

Beat at low speed with electric mixer for ½ minute, scraping sides of bowl constantly. Beat 3 minutes at high speed. By hand, stir in whole wheat flour and enough of the remaining un-bleached white flour to make a moderately stiff dough. Turn dough out onto lightly floured sur-face and knead till smooth and elastic (8 to 10 minutes). Shape in a ball. Place ball of dough in lightly greased bowl, turning once to grease surface. Cover and let rise in warm place until double (about 45 to 60 minutes).

Punch dough down; turn out on lightly floured surface. Divide in half. Cover; let rest 10 minutes. Shape *each half* into a loaf and place in greased 8½x4½x2½-inch loaf pans. Cover and let rise in warm place until double (30 to 45 minutes). Bake at 375° for 30 to 35 minutes. If crusts brown too quickly, cover loosely with foil the last 15 minutes. Remove loaves from pans and cool on wire rack. Brush tops with melted butter, if desired. Makes 2 loaves.

WHEAT GERM BREAD

6¼ to 6½ cups unbleached white flour
½ cup nonfat dry milk powder
1 package active dry yeast
¼ cup sugar
3 tablespoons cooking oil
½ cup whole wheat flour
¼ cup wheat germ

In large mixer bowl combine *3½ cups* of the un-bleached white flour, dry milk powder, and yeast. Heat 2¾ cups water, sugar, oil, and 2 teaspoons salt till warm (115-120°). Add to dry mixture. Beat at low speed with mixer for ½ minute, scraping bowl. Beat 3 minutes at high speed. By hand, stir in whole wheat flour, wheat germ, and enough remaining unbleached white flour to make a moderately stiff dough.

Knead on floured surface till smooth (5 to 8 minutes). Shape in ball. Place in greased bowl; turn once. Cover; let rise in warm place till double (40 to 50 minutes). Punch down; divide in half. Cover; let rest 10 minutes. Shape in two loaves; place in two greased 8½x4½x2½-inch loaf pans. Cover and let rise till double (about 30 minutes). Bake at 375° for 30 to 35 minutes. Remove from pans and cool. Makes 2 loaves.

BRAN BREAD

In large mixer bowl combine 1½ cups un-bleached white flour and 1 package active dry yeast. Heat ¾ cup milk, 2 tablespoons packed brown sugar, 2 tablespoons honey, 2 table-spoons butter or margarine, and 1 teaspoon salt till warm (115-120°), stirring constantly to melt butter. Add to dry mixture in bowl; add 1 egg.

Beat at low speed with electric mixer for ½ minute, scraping bowl constantly. Beat 3 min-utes at high speed. By hand, stir in 1 cup whole bran cereal and 1 to 1¼ cups unbleached white flour to make a stiff dough. Turn out on lightly floured surface and knead till smooth and elas-tic (5 to 8 minutes). Shape in ball.

Place in greased bowl, turning once. Cover; let rise in warm place till double (about 2 hours). Punch down. Cover; let rest 10 minutes. Shape in loaf; place in greased 8½x4½x2½-inch loaf pan. Cover; let rise till double (about 1 hour). Bake at 375° for 30 to 35 minutes. Remove from pan and cool. Makes 1 loaf.

SWISS OATMEAL BREAD

4½ to 4¾ cups unbleached white flour
2 cups rolled oats
2 packages active dry yeast
2 cups milk
¼ cup packed brown sugar
¼ cup butter or margarine
1 cup shredded Swiss cheese (4 ounces)

In large mixer bowl combine *1½ cups* of the flour, rolled oats, and yeast. Heat milk, brown sugar, butter, and 2 teaspoons salt till warm (115-120°), stirring constantly to melt butter. Add to dry mixture. Beat at low speed with mixer for ½ minute, scraping bowl. Beat 3 min-utes at high speed. By hand, stir in cheese and enough remaining flour to make a soft dough.

Knead on a floured surface till smooth and elastic (about 10 minutes). Shape in ball. Place in greased bowl; turn once. Cover; let rise till double (about 1 hour). Punch down; divide in half. Cover; let rest 10 minutes. Shape into two loaves and place in two greased 8½x4½x2½-inch loaf pans. Cover and let rise till double (about 30 minutes). Bake at 350° about 50 min-utes. Cover loosely with foil last 25 minutes. Remove from pans; cool. Makes 2 loaves.

BARLEY FLOUR BATTER BREAD

2½ cups unbleached white flour
1 package active dry yeast
⅓ cup light molasses
¼ cup butter or margarine
1 egg
¾ cup barley flour

In small mixer bowl combine *1½ cups* of the unbleached flour and the yeast. Heat 1 cup water, molasses, butter, and 2 teaspoons salt till warm (115-120°), stirring constantly. Add to dry mixture; add egg. Beat at low speed with elec-tric mixer for ½ minute, scraping bowl.

Beat 3 minutes at high speed. By hand, stir in barley flour and enough remaining white flour to make soft dough. Cover; let rise till double (45 to 60 minutes). Spread in greased 9x5x3-inch loaf pan; smooth top. Cover; let rise till double (30 to 45 minutes). Bake at 375° for 25 to 30 minutes. Cover with foil last 15 minutes. Remove from pan; cool. Makes 1 loaf.

PILGRIMS' BREAD

½ cup yellow cornmeal
⅓ cup packed brown sugar
1 tablespoon salt
2 cups boiling water
¼ cup cooking oil
2 packages active dry yeast
½ cup warm water (110°)
¾ cup whole wheat flour
½ cup rye flour
4¼ to 4½ cups unbleached white flour

Thoroughly combine cornmeal, brown sugar, and salt; stir gradually into boiling water. Stir in oil. Cool to lukewarm (about 30 minutes). Soften yeast in the warm water; stir into cornmeal mixture. Add whole wheat and rye flours; mix well. By hand, stir in enough unbleached white flour to make a moderately stiff dough. Turn out onto a lightly floured surface; knead till smooth and elastic (6 to 8 minutes).

Shape dough into a ball. Place in lightly greased bowl, turning once to grease surface. Cover and let rise in warm place until double (50 to 60 minutes). Punch dough down; turn out onto lightly floured surface and divide in half. Cover; let rest 10 minutes.

Shape the dough into two loaves and place in two greased 9x5x3-inch loaf pans. Cover and let the shaped loaves rise in a warm place until almost double (about 30 minutes). Bake the loaves at 375° till done, about 45 minutes. (If bread browns rapidly, cap loosely with foil after first 25 minutes.) Remove bread from pans and cool on wire racks. Makes 2 loaves.

Sample the natural flavors of whole wheat and rye flours plus yellow cornmeal in *Pilgrims' Bread.* This crusty loaf is especially good sliced thick and generously buttered or toasted for sandwiches.

Sourdough Starter

Soften 1 package active dry yeast in ½ cup *warm* water (110°). Stir in 2 cups *warm* water, 2 cups all-purpose flour, and 1 tablespoon sugar. Beat till smooth. Cover with cheesecloth; let stand at room temperature 5 to 10 days, stirring 2 to 3 times a day. (Time required to ferment depends on room temperature; if room is warm, let stand a shorter time than if room is cool.) Cover and refrigerate till ready to use.

To keep Starter going: After using some Starter, add ¾ cup water, ¾ cup all-purpose flour, and 1 teaspoon sugar to remainder. Let stand at room temperature till bubbly, at least 1 day. Cover and refrigerate for later use. If not used within 10 days, add 1 teaspoon sugar. Repeat adding sugar every 10 days.

SOURDOUGH BREAD

    1 package active dry yeast
 1½ cups warm water (110°)
 5½ to 6 cups all-purpose flour
    1 cup Sourdough Starter (room temp.)
    2 teaspoons salt
    2 teaspoons sugar
    ½ teaspoon baking soda

In large mixer bowl soften yeast in warm water. Blend in 2½ *cups* of the flour, Sourdough Starter, salt, and sugar. Combine 2½ *cups* of the flour and the baking soda; stir into flour-yeast mixture. Add enough remaining flour to make a stiff dough. Turn out onto a lightly floured surface and knead till smooth and elastic (5 to 7 minutes). Shape in ball. Place in greased bowl; turn once. Cover and let rise in warm place till double (about 1½ hours). Punch down; divide in half.

Cover and let rest 10 minutes. Shape into 2 round loaves. Place on lightly greased baking sheets. With sharp knife, make diagonal slashes across tops of loaves. Let rise in warm place till double (1 to 1½ hours). Bake at 400° for 35 to 40 minutes. Remove from baking sheets; cool. If desired, brush with butter. Makes 2 loaves.

SOURDOUGH ENGLISH MUFFINS

    1 cup Sourdough Starter (room temp.)
    ¾ cup buttermilk
 2¾ cups all-purpose flour
    6 tablespoons yellow cornmeal
    1 teaspoon baking soda
    ¼ teaspoon salt

Mix together Sourdough Starter and buttermilk. Combine flour, *4 tablespoons* of the cornmeal, soda, and salt; add to buttermilk mixture. Stir to combine well. Turn out onto lightly floured surface and knead till smooth and elastic, adding more flour if necessary. Roll dough to ⅜-inch thickness. Let rest a few minutes.

Using a 3-inch cutter, cut dough into muffins. Sprinkle sheet of waxed paper with *1 tablespoon* of the cornmeal; place muffins atop, and sprinkle with the remaining cornmeal. Cover and let rise till very light (about 45 minutes). Bake on medium-hot, lightly greased griddle about 30 minutes, turning often. Cool. Split; toast and serve with butter. Makes 12 to 14.

SOURDOUGH-CORNMEAL BREAD

    1 package active dry yeast
    6 cups unbleached white flour
    1 cup Sourdough Starter (room temp.)
    ¼ cup honey
    3 tablespoons butter, softened
 1½ cups yellow cornmeal
    ½ teaspoon baking soda
      Yellow cornmeal

In large mixer bowl soften yeast in 1½ cups *warm* water (110°). Blend in *3 cups* of the unbleached flour, Sourdough Starter, honey, butter, and 1 tablespoon salt. Beat 3 to 4 minutes with electric mixer. Combine 1½ cups cornmeal and soda; stir into flour-yeast mixture. Stir in enough remaining flour to make a moderately stiff dough. Knead on lightly floured surface till smooth (8 to 10 minutes). Shape in ball.

Place in greased bowl; turn once. Cover; let rise in warm place till double (about 1½ hours). Divide in half. Cover; let rest 10 minutes. Shape into 2 loaves and place in two greased 8½x4½x 2½-inch loaf pans sprinkled with cornmeal. Cover; let rise till double (45 to 60 minutes). Bake at 375° for 35 to 40 minutes. Makes 2 loaves.

SOURDOUGH-WHEAT BREAD

1 package active dry yeast
3 cups whole wheat flour
1 cup Sourdough Starter (room temp.)
¼ cup dark molasses
3 tablespoons butter, softened
2½ to 3 cups unbleached white flour
½ teaspoon baking soda

In large mixer bowl soften yeast in 1½ cups *warm* water (110°). Blend in whole wheat flour, Sourdough Starter, molasses, butter, and 2 teaspoons salt. Combine *1 cup* of the white flour and soda; stir into flour-yeast mixture. Add enough remaining unbleached flour to make a moderately stiff dough. Knead on floured surface till smooth (5 to 8 minutes). Shape in ball.

Place in greased bowl, turning once. Cover and let rise till double (1½ to 2 hours). Punch down; divide in half. Cover; let rest 10 minutes. Shape in 2 loaves; place in two greased 8½x 4½x2½-inch loaf pans. Cover; let rise till double (about 1 hour). Bake at 375° for 35 to 40 minutes. Remove from pans; cool. Makes 2 loaves.

SOURDOUGH-RYE BREAD

1 package active dry yeast
3 cups rye flour
1 cup Sourdough Starter (room temp.)
¼ cup sugar
3 tablespoons butter, softened
2 teaspoons caraway seed
3 to 3¼ cups unbleached white flour
½ teaspoon baking soda

In large mixer bowl soften yeast in 1½ cups *warm* water (110°). Blend in rye flour, Sourdough Starter, sugar, butter, caraway seed, and 2 teaspoons salt; beat well. Combine *1 cup* of the white flour and the soda; stir into flour-yeast mixture. Add enough remaining unbleached flour to make a moderately stiff dough. Knead on floured surface till smooth (5 to 8 minutes).

Place in greased bowl, turning once. Cover; let rise till double (about 1½ hours). Punch down; divide in half. Cover; let rest 10 minutes. Shape in 2 loaves; place in greased 8½x4½x2½-inch loaf pans. Cover; let rise till almost double (45 minutes). Bake at 375° for 35 to 40 minutes. Remove from pans; cool. Makes 2 loaves.

SOURDOUGH FRENCH BREAD

1 package active dry yeast
5 to 5½ cups all-purpose flour
1 cup Sourdough Starter (room temp.)
3 tablespoons sugar
2 tablespoons butter, melted
½ teaspoon baking soda
   Yellow cornmeal

In large mixer bowl soften yeast in 1½ cups *warm* water (110°). Blend in *2 cups* of the flour, Sourdough Starter, sugar, butter, and 2 teaspoons salt. Combine *1 cup* of the flour and the soda; stir into flour-yeast mixture. Add enough remaining flour to make a moderately stiff dough. Knead on floured surface till smooth (5 to 8 minutes). Place in greased bowl; turn once. Cover; let rise till double (1 to 1½ hours).

Punch down; divide in half. Cover; let rest 10 minutes. Shape in 2 oblong or round loaves. Place on greased baking sheet sprinkled with cornmeal. Cover; let rise till almost double (about 1 hour). Brush with water and make diagonal slashes across tops. Bake at 375° for 30 to 35 minutes. Remove from sheet; cool. Makes 2.

SOURDOUGH-CHEESE ROLLS

1 package active dry yeast
4¼ to 4½ cups unbleached white flour
1 cup Sourdough Starter (room temp.)
¼ cup sugar
¼ cup butter or margarine, softened
1 egg
½ teaspoon baking soda
¾ cup grated sharp Cheddar cheese

In large mixer bowl soften yeast in ¾ cup *warm* water (110°). Blend in *2 cups* of the flour, Sourdough Starter, sugar, butter, egg, and 2 teaspoons salt. Beat 3 to 4 minutes with mixer. Add soda to *1 cup* of the flour; stir into flour-yeast mixture. Add cheese and enough remaining flour to make a soft dough. Knead on floured surface till smooth (5 to 8 minutes).

Place in greased bowl; turn once. Cover; let rise till double (1½ to 2 hours). Punch down. Cover; let rest 10 minutes. Divide into 24 pieces; shape into balls. Place on greased baking sheets. Cover; let rise till double (25 to 30 minutes). Bake at 375° about 20 minutes. Makes 24 rolls.

Foreign and Holiday Breads

ITALIAN BREAD

    7¼ to 7¾ cups all-purpose flour
    2 packages active dry yeast
    2½ cups warm water (110°)
    1 tablespoon salt
    Yellow cornmeal
    1 slightly beaten egg white

In large mixer bowl combine *3 cups* of the flour and the yeast. Combine warm water and salt. Add to dry mixture in mixer bowl. Beat at low speed with electric mixer for ½ minute, scraping sides of bowl constantly. Beat 3 minutes at high speed. By hand, stir in enough of the remaining flour to make a very stiff dough. Turn out on a lightly floured surface and knead till smooth and very elastic (15 to 25 minutes). Shape in a ball. Place dough in a lightly greased bowl, turning once to grease surface. Cover and let dough rise in a warm place till double (1¼ to 1½ hours).

Punch dough down; turn out on lightly floured surface. Divide in half. Cover; let rest 10 minutes. Shape (directions follow recipe).

Place on greased baking sheets sprinkled with cornmeal. Cover and let shaped loaves rise in warm place till double (45 to 60 minutes). When ready to bake, place a large shallow pan on lower rack of oven and fill with boiling water. Add 1 tablespoon water to egg white; brush over top and sides of loaves.

Bake large loaves (round, long, or plump) at 375° about 20 minutes; brush again with egg white mixture. Bake about 20 minutes longer. Bake small breads (individual loaves or hard rolls) at 400° about 15 minutes. Brush again with egg white mixture. Bake 10 to 15 minutes longer. Cool on wire racks. Makes 2 Round Loaves; *or* 2 Long Loaves; *or* 2 Plump Loaves; *or* 8 Individual Loaves; *or* 16 Hard Rolls.

Round Loaves: Shape each half of dough into a round ball; place balls on large greased baking sheet sprinkled with cornmeal. With sharp knife, score loaves, making 3 shallow cuts, 1 inch apart, across top. Then, make 3 crosswise cuts. Follow recipe to brush, rise, and bake.

Long Loaves: Roll each half of dough to a 15x12-inch rectangle. Beginning at long side of rectangle, roll dough up tightly, sealing well as you roll. Taper ends of loaf. Place each loaf diagonally, seam side down, on greased baking sheet sprinkled with cornmeal. With sharp knife, make diagonal cuts, 2½ inches apart (⅛ to ¼ inch deep), on tops of loaves. Follow recipe directions to brush, rise, and bake.

Plump Loaves: Roll each half of dough to a 15x 8-inch rectangle. Beginning at short side of rectangle, roll dough up tightly, sealing well as you roll. Taper ends by rolling with hands till loaf measures 10 to 11 inches in length. Place loaves, seam side down, on greased baking sheet sprinkled with cornmeal. With sharp knife, gently make lengthwise cut, ¼ to ½ inch deep, down center of each loaf. Follow recipe directions to brush, rise, and bake.

Individual Loaves: Cut each half of dough in quarters, making 8 pieces. Round each piece of dough in a ball. Cover and let rest 10 minutes. Shape each ball of dough in a small loaf, twisting and pulling ends to taper. (Loaf should measure about 6 inches in length.) Place 2 to 3 inches apart on greased baking sheet sprinkled with cornmeal. Press down ends of loaves. With sharp knife, gently make 3 shallow cuts diagonally across top of each loaf. Follow recipe directions to brush, rise, and bake.

Hard Rolls: Divide each half of dough in eighths, making 16 pieces in all. Shape each piece in an oval or round roll; place about 2 inches apart on greased baking sheet sprinkled with cornmeal. Cut shallow crisscross in top of each roll. Follow recipe to brush, rise, and bake.

A foreign bread shaped five ways

Using the basic recipe for *Italian Bread*, you can →
mold the dough into any of the following shapes—
Round Loaves, Long Loaves, Plump Loaves,
Individual Loaves, or round Hard Rolls.

Serve warm *Syrian Bread* with butter. Or, make sandwiches by filling the centers with chopped tomato, shredded lettuce, and sliced onion.

FINNISH VIIPURI TWIST

5½ to 5¾ cups all-purpose flour
2 packages active dry yeast
½ teaspoon ground cardamom
½ teaspoon ground nutmeg
2 cups milk
¾ cup sugar
¼ cup butter or margarine
1 slightly beaten egg

In large mixer bowl combine 2½ *cups* of the flour, yeast, cardamom, and nutmeg. In saucepan heat milk, sugar, butter, and 1 teaspoon salt till warm (115-120°), stirring constantly to melt butter. Add to dry mixture. Beat at low speed with mixer for ½ minute, scraping bowl. Beat 3 minutes at high speed. By hand, stir in enough remaining flour to make a moderately stiff dough. Knead till smooth (5 to 8 minutes). Place in greased bowl, turning once. Cover; let rise till double (1 to 1½ hours). Punch down.

Divide in thirds. Cover; let rest 10 minutes. On floured surface shape one part into a roll 36 inches long. Cross ends to form a circle, extending each end about 6 inches. Holding ends toward center of circle, twist together twice. Press ends together and tuck under center of top of circle, forming a pretzel-shaped roll. Place on greased baking sheet. Repeat with remaining dough. Let rise till almost double (about 45 minutes). Bake at 375° about 20 minutes. Combine egg and 1 tablespoon water; brush on hot breads. Makes 3 loaves.

SYRIAN BREAD

5 to 5½ cups all-purpose flour 2½ - 3
2 packages active dry yeast 1 pkg.
• • •
2 cups milk 1 c.
3 tablespoons sugar 1½ TSP
3 tablespoons shortening 1½ TSP
2 teaspoons salt 1 tsp

In large mixer bowl combine 2 *cups* of the flour and the yeast. Heat milk, sugar, shortening, and 2 teaspoons salt just till warm (115-120°), stirring constantly to melt shortening. Add to dry mixture. Beat at low speed with electric mixer for ½ minute, scraping bowl. Beat 3 minutes at high speed. By hand, stir in enough remaining flour to make a moderately stiff dough.

Knead on floured surface till smooth. Place in greased bowl; turn once. Cover; let rise till double (40 to 45 minutes). Punch down; cover and let rest 10 minutes. Form into balls 1½ inches in diameter. Place on *ungreased* baking sheets; roll each to a 4-inch circle. Bake at 400° till puffed, 7 to 9 minutes. Cool on cloth-covered surface. Makes about 32 rolls.

SALLY LUNN

1 package active dry yeast
¾ cup warm milk (110°)
6 tablespoons butter or
    margarine
3 tablespoons sugar
• • •
2 eggs
3 cups all-purpose flour
1¼ teaspoons salt

Soften yeast in ¼ cup *warm* water (110°). Add milk and set aside. Cream butter and sugar. Add eggs, one at a time, beating after each addition. Combine flour and 1¼ teaspoons salt; add to creamed mixture alternately with yeast mixture. Beat well after each addition.

Beat till smooth. Cover; let rise till double (about 1 hour). Beat down and pour into well-greased Turk's head mold or 9-inch tube pan. Let rise till double (about 30 minutes). Bake at 350° for 40 to 45 minutes. Remove the coffee cake from the pan; serve it either warm or cold. Makes 1 coffee cake.

CARDAMOM BRAID

In large mixer bowl combine 1 cup all-purpose flour, 1 package active dry yeast, and ¾ teaspoon ground cardamom. Heat ¾ cup milk, ⅓ cup sugar, ¼ cup butter or margarine, and ½ teaspoon salt till warm (115-120°), stirring constantly to melt butter. Add to dry mixture; add 1 egg. Beat at low speed with electric mixer for ½ minute, scraping bowl. Beat 3 minutes at high speed. By hand, stir in 1¾ to 2 cups all-purpose flour to make a moderately soft dough.

Turn out on floured surface, knead till smooth (5 to 8 minutes). Place in greased bowl; turn once. Cover; let rise till double (about 1¼ hours). Punch down. Divide in thirds; form into balls. Cover; let rest 10 minutes. Roll each ball to a 16-inch rope. Line up the 3 ropes, 1 inch apart, on greased baking sheet.

Braid loosely *(see tip, page 38).* Pinch ends together and tuck under. Cover; let rise in warm place till almost double (about 40 minutes). Brush with milk and sprinkle with 1 tablespoon sugar. Bake at 375° for 20 to 25 minutes. Remove from baking sheet; cool. Makes 1 braid.

CHRISTMAS KRINGLE

   ¾ cup butter or margarine, softened
   1 package active dry yeast
   1 slightly beaten egg
   ¾ cup cold milk
   ¼ cup sugar
   1 teaspoon salt
   3 cups all-purpose flour
   1 egg
   Sweet Filling
   ¼ cup finely chopped blanched almonds
   ¼ cup sugar

Roll butter out between sheets of waxed paper to 10x6-inch rectangle. Chill. Soften yeast in ¼ cup *warm* water (110°). In large mixer bowl combine beaten egg, milk, ¼ cup sugar, and salt. Stir in softened yeast and flour; mix well to form a moderately stiff dough.

Roll out on floured surface to 12-inch square; place chilled butter in center. Fold sides of dough over to cover butter, forming a 12x6-inch rectangle; pinch to seal center seam and ends. Cover; let rest 10 minutes. Roll out again to 12-inch square; fold in thirds. Wrap in foil and chill 30 to 60 minutes. Repeat rolling, chilling, and folding twice more. Cut lengthwise into 3 strips, 12 inches long. Roll first strip to 18x4-inch rectangle. Combine egg and 1 tablespoon water; brush some on rectangle. Sprinkle with ⅓ of the Sweet Filling. Seal edges together to form an 18-inch-long roll. Place, seam side down, on greased baking sheet, shaping roll into an oval. Seal ends together and flatten to ½-inch thickness.

Brush surface with egg-water mixture and sprinkle with some of the chopped almonds and some of the ¼ cup sugar. Repeat with remaining dough and filling to make 2 more ovals. Let rest for 30 minutes. Bake at 375° about 25 minutes. Remove from baking sheets; cool. Makes 3.

Sweet Filling: Cream ½ cup butter and 1½ cups sugar till fluffy. Stir in 1½ cups light raisins *or* 1½ cups coarsely chopped pecans.

SWEDISH LIMPA BREAD

   3½ to 4 cups all-purpose flour
   2 packages active dry yeast
   2 teaspoons caraway seed
   ½ teaspoon fennel seed (optional)
   2 cups milk
   ½ cup packed brown sugar
   2 tablespoons molasses
   2 tablespoons butter or margarine
   2 tablespoons grated orange peel
   2½ cups rye flour

In large mixer bowl combine 2½ *cups* of the all-purpose flour, yeast, caraway seed, and fennel seed, if desired. Heat milk, brown sugar, molasses, butter, and 2 teaspoons salt till warm (115-120°), stirring constantly to melt butter. Add to dry mixture; add orange peel. Beat at low speed with mixer for ½ minute, scraping bowl. Beat 3 minutes at high speed. By hand, stir in rye flour and enough remaining all-purpose flour to make a moderately stiff dough.

Knead on lightly floured surface till smooth (8 to 10 minutes). Shape into ball. Place in greased bowl; turn once. Cover; let rise till double (1 to 1½ hours). Punch down; divide in half. Cover; let rest 10 minutes. Shape in 2 round loaves; place in greased 8-inch pie plates or on greased baking sheets. Cover; let rise till double (about 45 minutes). Bake at 375° about 30 minutes. Remove from pans; cool. Makes 2.

FRENCH BREAD

Pictured with Croissants and Raisin Brioche Ring at the beginning of this section (page 54)—

- **7 to 7¼ cups all-purpose flour**
- **2 packages active dry yeast**
- **1 tablespoon sugar**
- **1 tablespoon shortening**
- **Yellow cornmeal**
- **1 egg white**

In large mixer bowl combine *3 cups* of the flour and the yeast. Heat 2½ cups water, sugar, 1 tablespoon salt, and shortening just till warm (115-120°), stirring constantly to melt shortening. Add to dry mixture. Beat at low speed with electric mixer for ½ minute, scraping bowl. Beat 3 minutes at high speed. By hand, stir in enough remaining flour to make a soft dough.

Knead on floured surface till smooth (10 to 12 minutes). Shape into ball. Place in greased bowl; turn once. Cover; let rise till double (1 to 1½ hours). Punch down; divide in half. Cover; let rest 10 minutes. Roll each half to 15x12-inch rectangle. Roll up tightly from long side; seal well. Taper ends. Place each diagonally, seam side down, on greased baking sheet sprinkled with cornmeal. Gash tops diagonally every 2½ inches, ⅛ to ¼ inch deep.

Beat egg white just till foamy; add 1 tablespoon water. Brush tops and sides of loaves. Cover; let rise till double (about 1 hour). Bake at 375° till light brown, about 20 minutes. Brush again with egg white mixture. Bake 20 minutes longer. Remove from sheets; cool. Makes 2.

RAISIN BRIOCHE RING

Cover 1½ cups raisins with water; bring to boiling. Drain; set aside. Soften 2 packages active dry yeast in ½ cup *warm* water (110°). Heat 1 cup milk, ⅓ cup sugar, ¼ cup butter or margarine, and 2 teaspoons salt, stirring constantly to melt butter. In large bowl combine milk mixture, raisins, softened yeast, and 3 eggs.

Stir in 5½ to 6 cups all-purpose flour to make a moderately soft dough. Turn out onto floured surface; knead till smooth (about 5 minutes). Shape in ball. Place in greased bowl; turn once. Cover; let rise till double (45 to 60 minutes). Punch down. Cover; let rest 10 minutes. Set aside about ⅕ of the dough. Divide

remaining dough in half. Cut each half into 8 pieces; shape into balls. Place 8 balls against edge of each of two greased 9x1½-inch round baking pans. With kitchen shears, snip dough crisscross fashion in center of each ball.

With finger, make hole where cross intersects. Divide reserved dough into 16 pieces; shape into balls. Press small balls firmly into holes in larger balls. Cover; let rise till double (about 45 minutes). Combine 1 egg yolk and 1 tablespoon water; brush on bread. Bake at 350° 20 minutes. Remove from pans; cool. Makes 2.

CROISSANTS

- **1½ cups butter or margarine**
- **⅓ cup all-purpose flour**
- **2 packages active dry yeast**
- **¾ cup milk**
- **¼ cup sugar**
- **1 egg**
- **3¾ to 4¼ cups all-purpose flour**
- **1 egg yolk**
- **1 tablespoon milk**

Cream butter with ⅓ cup flour. Roll mixture between waxed paper to 12x6-inch rectangle. Chill 1 hour or longer. Soften yeast in ½ cup *warm* water (110°). Heat ¾ cup milk, sugar, and 1 teaspoon salt till sugar dissolves. Cool to lukewarm; turn into bowl. Add yeast mixture and 1 egg; beat. Stir in *2 cups* flour; beat. Stir in as much of remaining flour as you can mix in with spoon. On lightly floured surface knead in enough of remaining flour to make a moderately soft dough. Knead till smooth and elastic (8 to 10 minutes). Let rest 10 minutes.

Roll to 14-inch square. Place *chilled* butter on one half of dough. Fold over other half; seal edges. Roll to 21x12-inch rectangle; seal edges. Fold into thirds. Roll to 21x12-inch rectangle. Fold and roll twice more; seal edges. Chill after each rolling. Fold into thirds to 12x7 inches. Chill several hours or overnight.

Roll ¼ of dough to 12-inch circle. Cut into 12 wedges; roll each up loosely starting from wide edge. Repeat with remaining dough.

Place on *ungreased* baking sheets, point down; curve ends. Cover; let rise till double (30 to 45 minutes). Beat egg yolk with 1 tablespoon milk; brush on rolls. Bake at 375° for 12 to 15 minutes. Remove from sheets; cool. Makes 48.

BRIOCHE

1 package active dry yeast
½ cup butter or margarine
⅓ cup sugar
3½ cups all-purpose flour
½ cup milk
4 eggs

Soften yeast in ¼ cup *warm* water (110°). Thoroughly cream butter, ⅓ cup sugar, and ½ teaspoon salt. Add *1 cup* of the flour and the milk to creamed mixture. Beat 3 eggs and 1 egg yolk together (reserve egg white). Add softened yeast and eggs to creamed mixture; beat well. By hand stir in remaining 3 cups flour till smooth. Turn into greased bowl. Cover; let rise in warm place till double (about 2 hours). Refrigerate overnight; stir down. Turn out on floured surface. Divide dough into quarters; set one aside. Divide each of the remaining into 8 pieces, making a total of 24. Form each piece into a ball. With floured hands, tuck under cut edges. Place in greased muffin pans. Divide reserved dough into 24 pieces; shape into balls.

With floured finger, make indentation in each large ball. Press small balls into indentations. Cover; let rise till double (40 to 45 minutes). Blend reserved egg white and 1 tablespoon water; brush over rolls. Bake at 375° for 15 minutes, brushing again with egg mixture after 7 minutes. Makes 24.

Place large balls in greased muffin pans. Cut reserved dough into 4 wedges; divide each into 6 smaller pieces and shape into 24 balls.

With your thumb or a knife handle, make an indentation in the top of each large ball in muffin pans. Holes will hold the small balls upright.

For *Brioche*, set aside ¼ of the dough. Divide remaining dough into 6 pieces; form each into 4 balls. With floured hands, tuck under edges.

Brush holes lightly with water and press a small ball firmly into each indentation. Let rise; brush tops of rolls with egg white-sugar mixture. Bake.

GUGELHUPF

> 1 package active dry yeast
> ¼ cup butter or margarine
> ½ cup sugar
> 2 eggs
> ½ cup milk
> 2½ cups all-purpose flour
> ½ cup light raisins
> 1 teaspoon grated lemon peel
> 1 tablespoon butter, melted
> 3 tablespoons fine dry bread crumbs
>   Blanched whole almonds

Soften yeast in ¼ cup *warm* water (110°). In mixer bowl cream ¼ cup butter and sugar till light; add eggs one at a time, beating after each. Add yeast and milk. Stir together thoroughly flour and 1 teaspoon salt; add to creamed mixture. Beat at medium speed with electric mixer till smooth (about 2 minutes). By hand, stir in raisins and lemon peel. Cover; let rise in warm place till double (about 2 hours).

Meanwhile, prepare a 1½-quart fluted tube pan by brushing with melted butter and sprinkling with bread crumbs. Arrange almonds in a design in bottom. Stir down batter; spoon carefully into mold. Let rise till almost double (about 1 hour). Bake at 350° till done, about 25 minutes. Cool 10 minutes; remove mold. Makes 1.

GERMAN DARK RYE BREAD

In large mixer bowl combine 3 cups all-purpose flour, ¼ cup unsweetened cocoa powder, 2 packages active dry yeast, and 1 tablespoon caraway seed. Heat 2 cups water, ⅓ cup molasses, 2 tablespoons butter, 1 tablespoon sugar, and 1 tablespoon salt till warm (115-120°), stirring constantly to melt butter. Add to dry mixture.

Beat at low speed with electric mixer for ½ minute, scraping bowl. Beat 3 minutes at high speed. By hand, stir in 3 to 3½ cups rye flour

An elegant molded bread

← Serve your guests generous slices of *Gugelhupf* at your next tea or luncheon. Taste a fresh hint of lemon in this raisin-filled bread. It's the perfect choice to serve with coffee or tea.

to make a soft dough. Turn out onto lightly floured surface and knead till smooth (about 5 minutes). Cover; let rest 20 minutes. Punch down; divide in half. Shape in two round loaves; place on greased baking sheets. Brush surfaces with a little cooking oil. Slash tops with sharp knife. Cover; let rise in warm place till double (45 to 60 minutes). Bake at 400° for 25 to 30 minutes. Remove from baking sheets; cool. Makes 2.

GERMAN STOLLEN

> 4 to 4½ cups all-purpose flour
> 1 package active dry yeast
> ¼ teaspoon ground cardamom
> 1¼ cups milk
> ½ cup butter *or* margarine
> ¼ cup granulated sugar
> 1 slightly beaten egg
> 1 cup raisins
> ¼ cup chopped mixed candied fruits
>   and peels
> ¼ cup dried currants
> ¼ cup chopped blanched almonds
> 2 tablespoons finely shredded
>   orange peel
> 1 tablespoon finely shredded
>   lemon peel
>   Confectioners' Icing (see page 26)

Combine 2 *cups* flour, yeast, and cardamom. Heat milk, butter, sugar, and 1 teaspoon salt just till warm (115-120°) and butter is nearly melted; stir constantly. Add to flour mixture; add egg. Beat at low speed ½ minute; scrape bowl constantly. Beat 3 minutes at high speed. Stir in as much of remaining flour as you can mix in with spoon. Stir in fruits, nuts, and peels.

Turn out onto lightly floured surface. Knead in enough of the remaining flour to make a soft dough. Knead till smooth (5 to 8 minutes). Place in a greased bowl; turn once. Cover; let rise in a warm place till double (about 1¾ hours). Punch down; turn out onto lightly floured surface. Divide into thirds. Cover; let rest 10 minutes. Roll one third of dough to a 10x6-inch rectangle. Without stretching, fold the long side over to within 1 inch of opposite side; seal. Place on greased baking sheet; repeat with remaining dough. Cover; let rise till almost double (about 1 hour). Bake at 375° for 18 to 20 minutes. Glaze warm bread with icing. Makes 3.

SUGARPLUM BREAD

5 to 5¼ cups all-purpose flour
2 packages active dry yeast
½ teaspoon ground nutmeg
1⅓ cups milk
½ cup sugar
¼ cup shortening
2 eggs
½ teaspoon vanilla
1 cup raisins
1 cup chopped mixed candied fruits
  and peels
Confectioners' Icing (see page 26)

In large mixer bowl combine *2 cups* of the flour, yeast, and nutmeg. Heat milk, sugar, shortening, and 1½ teaspoons salt just till warm (115-120°), stirring constantly to melt shortening. Add to dry mixture; add eggs and vanilla. Beat at low speed with electric mixer for ½ minute, scraping bowl constantly. Beat 3 minutes at high speed. By hand, stir in raisins, fruits, and enough remaining flour to make a soft dough.

Knead on lightly floured surface till smooth (8 to 10 minutes). Shape into a ball. Place in greased bowl; turn once. Cover; let rise in warm place till double (about 1½ hours). Punch down; divide dough as specified in following shaping methods. Cover; let rest 10 minutes. Shape dough into Baby Sugarplums, Little Sugarplum Loaves, or Sugarplum Round Loaves.

Baby Sugarplums: Divide dough in fourths. Shape each fourth of the dough into 6 balls. Place in greased muffin pans. Cover and let rise in warm place till almost double (about 45 minutes). Bake at 350° for 18 to 20 minutes. Remove from pans; cool. Drizzle with Icing. If desired, trim with a walnut half. Makes 24.

Little Sugarplum Loaves: Divide dough in eighths. Shape each piece into a loaf. Place in eight greased 4½x2½x1½-inch loaf pans. Cover; let rise in warm place till almost double (about 45 minutes). Bake at 350° for 20 to 25 minutes. Remove from pans; cool. Drizzle tops with Confectioners' Icing. Trim with red and green candied cherries, if desired. Makes 8.

Sugarplum Round Loaves: Divide dough in half. Shape into 2 balls. Place on greased baking sheets and pat tops to flatten slightly. Cover and let rise in warm place till double (about 2 hours). Bake at 350° about 30 minutes. Remove from sheets; cool on racks. Frost with Confectioners' Icing. If desired, decorate with red and green candied cherries. Makes 2 loaves.

JULEKAGE

4½ to 5 cups all-purpose flour
2 packages active dry yeast
¾ teaspoon ground cardamom
1¼ cups milk
½ cup sugar
½ cup butter or margarine
1 teaspoon salt
1 egg
1 cup chopped mixed candied fruits
1 cup light raisins
1 slightly beaten egg yolk
  Confectioners' Icing (see page 26)

In large mixer bowl combine *2½ cups* of the flour, yeast, and cardamom. In saucepan heat milk, sugar, butter, and salt just till warm (115-120°), stirring constantly to melt butter. Add to dry mixture in mixer bowl; add 1 egg. Beat at low speed with electric mixer for ½ minute, scraping bowl. Beat 3 minutes at high speed. By hand, stir in fruits, raisins, and enough remaining flour to make a soft dough.

Turn out on lightly floured surface and knead till smooth (8 to 10 minutes). Shape into ball. Place in greased bowl, turning once. Cover; let rise in warm place till double (1¼ to 1½ hours). Punch down; divide in half. Cover; let rest 10 minutes. Shape in two loaves; place in two greased 9x5x3-inch loaf pans. Cover; let rise in warm place till double (about 45 minutes).

Combine egg yolk with 2 tablespoons water; brush over loaves. Bake at 350° for 35 to 40 minutes. Remove from pans; cool. Drizzle with Icing. Garnish with almonds and red and green candied cherries, if desired. Makes 2.

Assortment of holiday breads

Make the holiday season festive with large →
Sugarplum Round Loaves, walnut-topped *Baby Sugarplums,* and *Little Sugarplum Loaves.* Serve them to your family or give them as gifts.

CHALLAH

    2 packages active dry yeast
    ¾ cup milk
    ¼ cup butter or margarine
    2 tablespoons sugar
       Dash powdered saffron (optional)
    4½ to 5 cups all-purpose flour
    2 eggs
    1 egg yolk
    1 tablespoon poppy seed

Soften yeast in ½ cup *warm* water (110°). Heat milk, butter, sugar, 2 teaspoons salt, and saffron till sugar dissolves; cool to lukewarm. Stir in *2 cups* of the flour; beat well. Add softened yeast and the 2 eggs; beat well. Stir in enough of the remaining flour to make a soft dough. Knead on floured surface till smooth and elastic (8 to 10 minutes). Shape into ball.

   Place in greased bowl; turn once. Cover; let rise in warm place till double (about 1¼ hours). Punch down; divide in thirds. Cover; let rest 10 minutes. Roll each third into an 18-inch strand; braid strands and secure ends *(see tip, page 38)*. Place on greased baking sheet. Cover; let rise till double (about 30 minutes). Brush with egg yolk combined with 1 tablespoon water; sprinkle with poppy seed. Bake at 375° for 45 to 50 minutes. Makes 1 braid.

HAMANTASCHEN

    1 package active dry yeast
    1 cup milk
    ¾ cup sugar
    ½ cup butter or margarine
    5 to 5½ cups all-purpose flour
    2 eggs
       Prune or Lemon-Poppy Seed Filling
    1 egg yolk

Soften yeast in ¼ cup *warm* water (110°). Heat milk, sugar, butter, and 1 teaspoon salt till sugar dissolves; cool to lukewarm. Stir in *2 cups* of the flour; beat well. Add softened yeast and 2 eggs; beat well. Stir in enough flour to make a moderately stiff dough.

   Knead on floured surface till smooth (8 to 10 minutes). Shape into ball. Place in greased bowl; turn once. Cover and let rise till double (1¼ to 1½ hours). Divide in half. Roll each half

to a 17x12-inch rectangle. Cut into 4-inch circles. Place Prune *or* Lemon-Poppy Seed Filling in center of *each* circle. Moisten edges; bring sides up and pinch together, forming a triangular base. Place on greased baking sheets; cover and let rise till double (20 to 30 minutes). Brush tops with egg yolk combined with 1 tablespoon water. Bake at 350° for 15 to 20 minutes. Remove from sheets and cool. Makes 30.

   Prune Filling: Rinse 2 cups unpitted prunes (about 1 pound), and cover with water 1 inch above the fruit in saucepan. Cover and simmer gently for 10 to 20 minutes; drain. Remove the pits and chop prunes. Add ½ cup sugar, ½ cup chopped nuts, 1 teaspoon grated lemon peel, and 1 tablespoon lemon juice; mix well. Use about 1 tablespoon filling for each circle.

   Lemon-Poppy Seed Filling: Combine one 12-ounce can poppy seed filling, 1 teaspoon grated lemon peel, and 1 tablespoon lemon juice. Use about ½ tablespoon filling for each circle.

HOLIDAY SWEET DOUGH

    4½ to 4¾ cups all-purpose flour
    2 packages active dry yeast
    1¼ cups milk
    ½ cup sugar
    ¼ cup shortening
    2 teaspoons salt
    2 eggs
    1 teaspoon grated lemon peel
       Confectioners' Icing (see page 26)
          or Thin Sugar Glaze

In large mixer bowl combine *2 cups* of the flour and the yeast. In saucepan heat milk, sugar, shortening, and salt just till warm (115-120°), stirring constantly to melt shortening. Add to the dry mixture in mixer bowl; add eggs and grated lemon peel. Beat at low speed with electric mixer for ½ minute, scraping sides of bowl constantly. Beat 3 minutes at high speed. By hand, stir in enough of the remaining flour to make a moderately stiff dough.

   Turn out onto lightly floured surface and knead till smooth and elastic (8 to 10 minutes). Shape into a ball. Place in lightly greased bowl, turning once. Cover and let rise in warm place until double (1½ to 2 hours). Punch down. Cover; let rest 10 minutes. Shape dough as Twistrees, Poinsettias, or Twist Bunnies.

Twistrees: Divide dough in thirds. For each tree, roll one-third to 12x6-inch rectangle. Spread with 1 tablespoon butter; sprinkle with 1 tablespoon red or green sugar crystals. Fold in half to 12x3-inch rectangle. Cut into twelve 1-inch strips. Twist each one; arrange on greased baking sheet, with cut ends to center, in tree shape. Use 10 strips for branches and 1 strip for base. Cut remaining strip in half; use as top branches for tree. Repeat with remaining dough. Cover and let rise in warm place till double (30 to 45 minutes). Bake at 375° for 12 to 15 minutes. Remove from sheets and cool. Drizzle with Confectioners' Icing. Makes 3 trees.

Twist strips of dough and arrange in tree fashion to make *Twistrees.* Use eleven strips for the branches and one strip for the base of each tree.

Poinsettias: Divide dough in half. Roll half to 16x12-inch rectangle. Brush with melted butter. Mix ½ cup finely chopped mixed candied fruits and peels or snipped gumdrops and 3 tablespoons sugar; sprinkle over dough. Roll as for jelly roll, beginning with narrow end; seal edge. Cut roll in twelve 1-inch pieces. Reserve the two end pieces for the center. Place remaining slices, cut side down, on greased baking sheet. Arrange in a circle around a 2-inch center space with each slice overlapping slightly.

Pinch outside edges of each slice to make petal tip. Divide each end piece in half; shape into balls. Place balls in center. Repeat with second half of dough. Cover; let rise in warm place till double (30 to 45 minutes). Bake at 350° for 15 to 18 minutes. Remove from sheets; cool. Glaze with Confectioners' Icing. If desired, decorate center with grated orange peel. Makes 2.

Overlap slices of candied fruit-filled dough in a circle to form *Poinsettias.* To form petal tips, pinch the outside edges of each slice.

Twist Bunnies: Roll dough to 15x12-inch rectangle. Cut dough in 24 strips, each 15 inches long and ½ inch wide. Snip 1 inch from end of each strip and reserve for tail. Roll long strip of dough between hands to smooth. On lightly greased baking sheet, overlap ends of long strip to form a circle at the bottom.

Bring underneath end up over top, leaving ends spread open to make ears. Pinch tips of ears into points. Form reserved piece of dough into small ball for tail; place atop dough at bottom of circle. Cover; let rise till almost double (30 to 45 minutes). Bake at 375° for 10 to 12 minutes. Remove from baking sheet. Frost while warm with Thin Sugar Glaze. Makes 24.

Thin Sugar Glaze: Combine 2 cups sifted powdered sugar, ¼ cup hot water, and 1 teaspoon softened butter; mix till well blended.

Make *Twist Bunnies* by overlapping and twisting a strip of dough. Spread the ends to make ears, and form the tail with a ball of dough.

MEXICAN HOLIDAY BREAD

    2 packages active dry yeast
    ¾ cup milk
    ½ cup butter or margarine
    ¼ cup sugar
    5¾ to 6¼ cups all-purpose flour
    3 eggs
    1 tablespoon grated orange peel
    1½ cups chopped candied cherries
    ½ cup chopped walnuts
       Confectioners' Icing (see page 26)

Soften yeast in ½ cup *warm* water (110°). Heat milk, butter, sugar, and 1 teaspoon salt till sugar dissolves; cool to lukewarm. Stir in *2 cups* of the flour; beat well. Add softened yeast, eggs, and peel; beat well. Stir in cherries, nuts, and enough remaining flour to make a moderately soft dough. Knead on floured surface till smooth (8 to 10 minutes). Shape into ball.

Place in greased bowl; turn once. Cover; let rise in warm place till double (about 1½ hours). Punch down; divide in half. Cover; let rest 10 minutes. Shape *each* in 20-inch roll and pinch ends together to form ring. Place in two greased 6½-cup ring molds. Cover; let rise till double (30 to 45 minutes). Bake at 375° for 20 to 25 minutes. Remove from molds; cool. Drizzle with Confectioners' Icing. If desired, decorate with candied fruits and nuts. Makes 2.

KOLACHE

    1 package active dry yeast
    ¾ cup milk
    ½ cup butter or margarine
    ¼ cup sugar
    3½ to 4¼ cups all-purpose flour
    ¼ teaspoon ground cinnamon
    2 eggs
    1 teaspoon grated lemon peel
       Prune Filling
       Sifted powdered sugar

Soften yeast in ¼ cup *warm* water (110°). Heat milk, butter, sugar, and 1 teaspoon salt till sugar dissolves; cool to lukewarm. Stir in *2 cups* of the flour and cinnamon; beat well. Add softened yeast, eggs, and peel; beat well. Stir in enough remaining flour to make a moderately soft dough. Knead on floured surface till smooth (8 to 10 minutes). Shape into ball. Place in greased bowl; turn once. Cover; let rise till double (1 to 1½ hours). Punch down; divide in half. Cover; let rest 10 minutes.

Shape *each half* in 9 balls. Place 3 inches apart on greased baking sheets. Flatten each to 3-inch circle. Cover; let rise till double (about 45 minutes). Make depression in center of each; fill with Prune Filling. Bake at 375° for 10 to 12 minutes. Remove from sheets; cool. Dust lightly with powdered sugar. Makes 18 rolls.

Prune Filling: In small saucepan combine 1 cup pitted prunes and enough water to come 1 inch above prunes. Simmer for 10 to 15 minutes; drain and chop prunes. Stir in ¼ cup sugar and ½ teaspoon ground cinnamon.

GREEK NEW YEAR'S BREAD

    5½ to 6 cups all-purpose flour
    2 packages active dry yeast
    1½ teaspoons grated lemon peel
    1 teaspoon crushed aniseed
    1½ cups milk
    6 tablespoons butter or margarine
    ⅓ cup sugar
    3 eggs
    1 slightly beaten egg yolk
    2 tablespoons sesame seed

In large mixer bowl combine *2 cups* of the flour, yeast, peel, and aniseed. Heat milk, butter, sugar, and 1 teaspoon salt till warm (115-120°), stirring constantly to melt butter. Add to dry mixture; add the 3 eggs. Beat at low speed with mixer for ½ minute, scraping bowl. Beat 3 minutes at high speed. By hand, stir in enough remaining flour to make a moderately stiff dough. Knead on lightly floured surface till smooth and elastic (8 to 10 minutes). Shape into ball.

Place in greased bowl; turn once. Cover; let rise till double (1 to 1½ hours). Punch down; divide in thirds. Cover; let rest 10 minutes. Shape *two* parts in flat, 8-inch round loaves. Place in two greased 9x1½-inch round baking pans. Divide third part in half; shape into two 18-inch strands. Twist each like a rope and seal ends to form two circles; place one atop each loaf. Combine yolk and 1 tablespoon water; brush on loaves. Sprinkle with sesame seed. Let rise till double (30 to 45 minutes). Bake at 375° about 25 minutes. Remove; cool. Makes 2.

ITALIAN PANETTONE

2 packages active dry yeast
½ cup milk
½ cup honey
½ cup butter or margarine
5½ to 6 cups all-purpose flour
3 eggs
½ cup light raisins
½ cup currants
¼ cup chopped citron
2 to 3 teaspoons crushed aniseed
1 egg

Soften yeast in ½ cup *warm* water (110°). Heat milk, honey, butter, and 1 teaspoon salt till butter melts; cool to lukewarm. Stir in *2 cups* of the flour; beat well. Add softened yeast and the 3 eggs; beat well. Stir in raisins, currants, citron, aniseed, and enough remaining flour to make a soft dough. Knead on floured surface till smooth (8 to 10 minutes).

Shape into ball. Place in greased bowl; turn once. Cover; let rise in warm place till double (about 1½ hours). Punch down; divide in half. Cover; let rest 10 minutes. Shape in 2 round loaves; place on two greased baking sheets. Cut a cross ½ inch deep on each loaf. Cover; let rise till double (about 45 minutes). Beat 1 egg with 1 tablespoon water; brush tops. Bake at 350° for 35 to 40 minutes. Remove from baking sheets; cool on racks. Makes 2 loaves.

GREEK HONEY-NUT BREAD

2½ to 3 cups all-purpose flour
1 package active dry yeast
¾ cup milk
¼ cup sugar
¼ cup butter or margarine
1 egg
½ teaspoon grated lemon peel
½ cup light raisins
½ cup chopped figs
½ cup chopped walnuts
¼ cup honey

In large mixer bowl combine *1 cup* of the flour and the yeast. Heat milk, sugar, butter, and ½ teaspoon salt just till warm (115-120°), stirring constantly to melt butter. Add to dry mixture; add egg and peel. Beat at low speed with elec- tric mixer for ½ minute, scraping bowl. Beat 3 minutes at high speed. By hand, stir in enough remaining flour to make a moderately stiff dough. Knead on floured surface till smooth (5 to 10 minutes). Shape into a ball.

Place in greased bowl; turn once. Cover; let rise till double (1 to 1½ hours). Knead in fruit and nuts. Let rest 10 minutes. Shape into round loaf; place in greased 9x1½-inch round baking pan. Let rise till double (about 45 minutes). Bake at 375° about 30 minutes. Remove from pan; brush with honey. Makes 1 loaf.

POLISH POPPY SEED ROLL

5 to 6 cups all-purpose flour
2 packages active dry yeast
1½ cups milk
⅓ cup sugar
⅓ cup shortening
3 eggs
Poppy Seed Filling

In large mixer bowl combine *2 cups* of the flour and the yeast. Heat milk, sugar, shortening, and 1 teaspoon salt till warm (115-120°), stirring constantly to melt shortening. Add to dry mix- ture; add eggs. Beat at low speed with electric mixer for ½ minute, scraping bowl. Beat 3 min- utes at high speed. By hand, stir in enough re- maining flour to make a moderately stiff dough.

Turn out on floured surface and knead till smooth and elastic (5 to 10 minutes). Shape into ball. Place in greased bowl; turn once. Cover; let rise in warm place till double (1 to 1¾ hours). Punch dough down; divide in half. Cover; let rest 10 minutes. On floured surface, roll *each* half to 24x8-inch rectangle; spread each with *half* the Poppy Seed Filling. Roll up, starting at short end; seal long ends. Place, seam side down, in greased 9x5x3-inch loaf pans. Cover; let rise till double (30 to 45 minutes). Bake at 350° for 35 to 40 minutes. Remove from pans; cool. Makes 2 loaves.

Poppy Seed Filling: Pour 1 cup boiling water over ¾ cup poppy seed (4 ounces); drain. Cover with 1 cup lukewarm water and let stand 30 minutes. Drain thoroughly. Grind the poppy seed in blender or use the finest blade of food grinder. Stir in ½ cup chopped nuts, ⅓ cup honey, and 1 teaspoon grated lemon peel. Fold 1 stiffly beaten egg white into filling mixture.

HOT CROSS BUNS

3½ to 4 cups all-purpose flour
2 packages active dry yeast
½ to 1 teaspoon ground cinnamon
¾ cup milk
½ cup cooking oil
⅓ cup sugar
3 eggs
⅔ cup dried currants
1 slightly beaten egg white
Frosting

In large mixer bowl combine *2 cups* of the flour, yeast, and cinnamon. Heat milk, oil, sugar, and ¾ teaspoon salt till warm (115-120°). Add to dry mixture; add eggs. Beat at low speed with electric mixer for ½ minute, scraping bowl. Beat 3 minutes at high speed. By hand, stir in currants and enough remaining flour to make a soft dough. Shape into ball. Place in greased bowl; turn once. Cover; let rise till double (about 1½ hours). Punch down. Cover; let rest 10 minutes.

Divide in 18 pieces; form smooth balls. Place on greased baking sheet 1½ inches apart. Cover; let rise till double (30 to 45 minutes). Cut shallow cross in each; brush tops with egg white

(reserve remaining). Bake at 375° for 12 to 15 minutes. Remove from sheet. Using pastry tube, pipe on crosses with Frosting. Makes 18 buns.

Frosting: Combine 1½ cups sifted powdered sugar, reserved egg white, ¼ teaspoon vanilla, and dash salt. Mix till smooth; add milk, if necessary, to make of piping consistency.

EASTER NEST COFFEE CAKE

1 package active dry yeast
½ cup milk
¼ cup sugar
¼ cup shortening
3 cups all-purpose flour
1 slightly beaten egg
Shredded coconut
Green food coloring
Confectioners' Icing (see page 26)
Candy decorations

Soften yeast in ¼ cup *warm* water (110°). Heat milk, sugar, shortening, and 1 teaspoon salt till sugar dissolves; cool to lukewarm. Stir in *1 cup* of the flour; beat smooth. Add softened yeast and egg; beat well. Stir in enough remaining flour to make a soft dough. Knead on lightly floured surface till smooth and elastic (8 to 10 minutes). Place in greased bowl; turn once. Cover; let rise in warm place till double (about 1 hour). Punch dough down; divide into thirds. Cover; let rest 10 minutes.

Shape ⅓ of dough into 6 'eggs'; place close together in center of greased baking sheet. For 'nest', shape remaining dough into two 26-inch ropes; twist together. Coil around 'eggs' (see photo at left); seal ends. Cover; let rise in warm place till double (about 1 hour). Bake at 375° for 15 to 20 minutes. Remove from sheet; cool. Tint coconut with a few drops of green food coloring. Frost coffee cake with Confectioners' Icing. Sprinkle 'eggs' with candy decorations and 'nest' with tinted coconut. Makes 1.

Group 'eggs' close together in the center of a greased baking sheet. Then, coil the twisted ropes of dough around the 'eggs'. Seal ends.

Eggs-in-a-basket Easter bread

Treat the kids on Easter morning to *Easter Nest Coffee Cake*, made from sweet bread dough. Sprinkle green-tinted coconut around the edge for grass and trim the 'eggs' with candies.

TEMPTING QUICK BREADS

When you're busy and there's no time to bake a yeast-leavened bread or coffee cake, or when your menu calls for some baking powder-leavened bread, look to this section. You'll find an assortment of recipes for biscuits, muffins, coffee cakes, and nut breads.

Quick breads, as the name implies, are easy to prepare and don't require time to rise—the dough expands during baking. Because they are simple to prepare, quick breads make great coffeetime or snacktime treats when you decide to have some friends over on the spur of the moment.

Many of the nut breads slice best if they are wrapped in foil or clear plastic wrap and stored overnight. However, coffee cakes, biscuits, and muffins are best when they are served hot from the oven.

The next time it's your turn to plan the refreshments, choose *Cranberry Muffins, Pumpkin-Nut Bread,* or *Peanut-Honey Coffee Cake.* (See index for page numbers.)

Biscuits and Muffins

BAKING POWDER BISCUITS

2 cups all-purpose flour
1 tablespoon baking powder
½ teaspoon salt
⅓ cup shortening
¾ cup milk

Stir thoroughly the flour, baking powder, and salt. Cut in shortening till mixture resembles coarse crumbs. Make a well in dry mixture; add milk all at once. Stir just till dough clings together. Knead gently on lightly floured surface (10 to 12 strokes). Roll or pat dough to ½-inch thickness. Cut with 2½-inch biscuit cutter; dip cutter in flour between cuts. Place on *ungreased* baking sheet. Bake at 450° till golden, 10 to 12 minutes. Makes 10 biscuits.

Buttermilk Biscuits: Prepare Baking Powder Biscuits as above, *except* add ¼ teaspoon baking soda to the flour mixture, and substitute buttermilk for milk in recipe. Makes 12 biscuits.

Drop Biscuits: Prepare Baking Powder Biscuits as above, *except* use 1 cup milk. Do not knead. Drop from tablespoon onto *ungreased* baking sheet. Bake as directed. Makes 12.

Whole Wheat Biscuits: Prepare Baking Powder Biscuits, *except* use 1½ cups all-purpose flour and ½ cup whole wheat flour. Makes 12.

PECAN TEA BISCUITS

In mixing bowl stir to combine thoroughly 1¾ cups all-purpose flour, 3 tablespoons sugar, 2 teaspoons baking powder, and ½ teaspoon salt. Cut in ¼ cup shortening till mixture resembles coarse crumbs. Combine 1 beaten egg and ¾ cup milk; add all at once to dry mixture, stirring just till dough clings together. Stir in ½ cup finely chopped pecans. Drop by heaping teaspoonfuls onto greased baking sheet. Combine 2 tablespoons sugar and ½ teaspoon ground cinnamon; sprinkle over biscuits. Bake at 425° for 8 to 10 minutes. Makes 36 biscuits.

BISCUITS SUPREME

Next time, sprinkle with toasted sesame seed—

2 cups all-purpose flour
4 teaspoons baking powder
1 tablespoon sugar
½ teaspoon cream of tartar
½ teaspoon salt
½ cup shortening
⅔ cup milk

Stir thoroughly the first 5 ingredients. Cut in shortening till mixture resembles coarse crumbs. Make a well in center; add milk all at once. Stir just till dough clings together. Knead gently on lightly floured surface (10 to 12 strokes). Roll or pat to ½-inch thickness. Dip 2½-inch biscuit cutter in flour; cut dough straight down. Bake on *ungreased* baking sheet at 450° for 10 to 12 minutes. Makes 12 biscuits.

OATMEAL DROP BISCUITS

1 cup all-purpose flour
1 tablespoon baking powder
¼ cup shortening
1 cup quick-cooking rolled oats
1 beaten egg
⅓ cup milk
2 tablespoons honey

Stir thoroughly the flour, baking powder, and ½ teaspoon salt. Cut in shortening till mixture resembles coarse crumbs. Stir in oats. Combine egg, milk, and honey; add all at once to dry mixture. Stir just till moistened. Drop by spoonfuls onto greased baking sheet. Bake at 425° for 8 to 10 minutes. Makes 12 biscuits.

Warm-from-the-oven biscuits

The wide variety of biscuits in this section are →
represented by flaky *Baking Powder Biscuits*,
Dixie Cornmeal Foldovers (recipe on page 85),
and *Cinnamon-Petal Biscuits* (recipe on page 84).

CINNAMON-PETAL BISCUITS

These fancy biscuits are pictured on page 83—

       2 cups all-purpose flour
       3 tablespoons sugar
       4 teaspoons baking powder
    ½ teaspoon cream of tartar
    ½ teaspoon salt
    ½ cup shortening
    ½ cup milk
       2 tablespoons butter, melted
    ¼ cup sugar
       1 to 1½ teaspoons ground cinnamon

Grease eight 2-inch-diameter muffin pans. Stir together the first 5 ingredients; cut in shortening till mixture resembles coarse crumbs. Add milk all at once; stir just till dough clings together. Knead gently on lightly floured surface (10 to 12 strokes). Roll to 15x8-inch rectangle, ¼ inch thick. Brush with butter. Combine ¼ cup sugar and cinnamon; sprinkle over surface. Cut into ten 8x1½-inch strips. Make 2 stacks of 5 strips each. Cut *each* stack into four 2x1½-inch pieces. Pressing layers together slightly, place biscuits, 1½-inch side down, in pans. Bake at 400° about 10 minutes. Cover with foil to prevent overbrowning; continue baking 18 minutes more. Makes 8 biscuits.

ONION-CELERY BISCUITS

    ¼ cup finely chopped onion
       1 tablespoon butter or margarine
    1½ cups all-purpose flour
    1½ teaspoons baking powder
    ½ teaspoon salt
    ½ teaspoon celery seed
    ¼ cup shortening
       1 beaten egg
    ⅓ cup milk

Cook onion in butter till tender. Stir thoroughly the flour, baking powder, salt, and celery seed. Cut in shortening till mixture resembles coarse crumbs. Add cooked onion, egg, and milk all at once; stir just till dough clings together. Knead gently on lightly floured surface (10 to 12 strokes). Roll or pat dough to ½-inch thickness. Cut with floured 2½-inch biscuit cutter. Bake on *ungreased* baking sheet at 425° for 12 to 13 minutes. Makes 12 biscuits.

TEA SCONES

A rich, British biscuit favorite—

       2 cups all-purpose flour
       2 tablespoons sugar
       1 tablespoon baking powder
    ½ teaspoon salt
             • • •
    ⅓ cup dried currants (optional)
       6 tablespoons butter or margarine
       1 beaten egg
    ½ cup milk
       1 slightly beaten egg

Stir thoroughly the flour, sugar, baking powder, and salt. Stir in currants, if desired. Cut in butter till mixture resembles coarse crumbs. Add 1 beaten egg and milk, stirring just till dough clings together. Knead gently on lightly floured surface (12 to 15 strokes). Cut dough in half. Shape *each half* into ball and pat or roll to 6-inch circle, about ½ inch thick. Cut *each* circle into 6 or 8 wedges. Place wedges on *ungreased* baking sheet (don't have sides touching). Brush scones with 1 slightly beaten egg. Bake at 425° till deep golden brown, 12 to 15 minutes. Makes 12 or 16 scones.

BUTTERMILK-BRAN SCONES

Bran flake cereal adds an interesting flavor—

       2 cups all-purpose flour
    ¼ cup sugar
       3 teaspoons baking powder
       1 teaspoon salt
    ½ teaspoon baking soda
             • • •
       2 cups bran flake cereal
    ½ cup dried currants
    ¼ cup butter or margarine
       2 beaten eggs
    ⅓ cup buttermilk

Stir thoroughly the flour, sugar, baking powder, salt, and soda. Stir in bran flake cereal and currants. Cut in butter till mixture resembles coarse crumbs. Stir in eggs and buttermilk. Knead gently on lightly floured surface (5 to 6 strokes). Divide dough in thirds. Roll *each third* into 5-inch circle, ½ inch thick; cut into 6 wedges. Bake on greased baking sheet at 400° about 15 minutes. Makes 18 scones.

Serve muffins warm

If you can't serve muffins immediately after baking, tip them to one side in pan to prevent crusts from becoming soggy. To rewarm muffins, wrap them in foil and heat at 400° for 15 to 20 minutes.

DIXIE CORNMEAL FOLDOVERS

These biscuits are shown on page 83 —

Stir thoroughly 1½ cups all-purpose flour, 1 tablespoon sugar, 2 teaspoons baking powder, ½ teaspoon baking soda, and ¼ teaspoon salt. Stir in ½ cup yellow cornmeal. Cut in ¼ cup shortening till mixture resembles coarse crumbs. Blend together 1 beaten egg and ¾ cup dairy sour cream; stir into dry mixture just till dough clings together. Knead gently on lightly floured surface (10 to 12 strokes).

Roll or pat dough to ¼-inch thickness; cut with floured 2½-inch biscuit cutter. Crease biscuits just off-center with back of knife; fold over so top portion overlaps bottom. Moisten edges with water; seal. Brush with 2 tablespoons melted butter. Bake on greased baking sheet at 425° for 8 to 10 minutes. Makes 20 to 24.

MUFFINS TROPICALE

    2 cups all-purpose flour
    2 teaspoons baking powder
    ½ teaspoon baking soda
    ½ teaspoon salt
    ½ cup packed brown sugar
    1 well-beaten egg
    1 cup dairy sour cream
    1 8¾-ounce can crushed pineapple
    ½ cup chopped pecans
    ⅓ cup cooking oil

Stir together thoroughly the flour, baking powder, baking soda, and salt; stir in brown sugar. Combine egg and sour cream. Stir in *undrained* pineapple, nuts, and oil; add to dry ingredients all at once. Stir till moistened. Fill greased muffin pans ⅔ full. Bake at 400° about 20 minutes. Makes 18 muffins.

PEANUT BUTTER MUFFINS

Dip warm muffins in sugar-cinnamon mixture —

    2 cups all-purpose flour
    ½ cup sugar
    3 teaspoons baking powder
    ½ teaspoon salt
    ½ cup chunk-style peanut butter
    2 tablespoons butter or margarine
    1 cup milk
    2 beaten eggs
        • • •
    2 tablespoons butter or margarine, melted
    ½ cup sugar
    2 teaspoons ground cinnamon

In mixing bowl stir to combine thoroughly the flour, ½ cup sugar, baking powder, and salt. Cut in chunk-style peanut butter and 2 tablespoons butter or margarine till mixture resembles coarse crumbs. Add milk and eggs all at once, stirring just till moistened. Fill greased muffin pans ⅔ full. Bake at 400° for 15 to 17 minutes. Immediately brush tops with the 2 tablespoons melted butter. Combine ½ cup sugar and cinnamon. Dip muffins in sugar mixture to coat tops. Serve hot. Makes 15 to 18.

FIG-OATMEAL MUFFINS

These tasty muffins are shown on page 4 —

    1 cup quick-cooking rolled oats
    1 cup milk
        • • •
    1 cup all-purpose flour
    ⅓ cup sugar
    1 tablespoon baking powder
    ½ teaspoon salt
        • • •
    1 well-beaten egg
    ¼ cup cooking oil
    ½ cup chopped dried figs

Combine quick-cooking rolled oats and milk; let stand 15 minutes. In mixing bowl stir to combine thoroughly the flour, sugar, baking powder, and salt. Combine egg, cooking oil, oat mixture, and dried figs; add all at once to dry ingredients. Stir just till dough clings together. Fill greased muffin pans ⅔ full. Bake at 400° for 18 to 20 minutes. Makes 12 muffins.

Plump, fresh blueberries and grated lemon peel give *Blueberry-Lemon Muffins* an extra-special flavor that will delight family and guests alike. They also are luscious made with frozen berries.

GINGER MUFFINS

Stir thoroughly 1½ cups all-purpose flour, 2 teaspoons baking powder, ¾ teaspoon salt, and ½ teaspoon *each* ground cinnamon and ground ginger. Cut in ¼ cup shortening till fine. Mix 1 beaten egg, ½ cup milk, and ½ cup molasses. Add to dry mixture; mix just till moistened. Fill greased muffin pans ⅔ full. Sprinkle with sugar. Bake at 400° about 20 minutes. Makes 9.

PUMPKIN MUFFINS

Stir thoroughly 1½ cups all-purpose flour, ½ cup sugar, 2 teaspoons baking powder, ¾ teaspoon salt, ½ teaspoon ground cinnamon, and ½ teaspoon ground nutmeg. Cut in ¼ cup shortening till fine. Combine 1 beaten egg, ½ cup canned pumpkin, and ½ cup milk; add to dry mixture and mix just till moistened. Stir in ½ cup light raisins. Fill greased muffin pans ⅔ full. Sprinkle additional sugar over each. Bake at 400° for 18 to 20 minutes. Makes 12 muffins.

APPLE MUFFINS

   1¾ cups all-purpose flour
    ¼ cup sugar
   2½ teaspoons baking powder
    ¾ teaspoon salt
    ½ teaspoon ground cinnamon
    1 well-beaten egg
    ¾ cup milk
    ⅓ cup cooking oil
    1 cup peeled and chopped apple
    2 tablespoons sugar
    ½ teaspoon ground cinnamon

Stir thoroughly first 5 ingredients; make well in center. Blend egg, milk, oil, and apple; add all at once to dry mixture. Stir just till moistened. Fill greased muffin pans ⅔ full. Sprinkle with mixture of the 2 tablespoons sugar and ½ teaspoon cinnamon. Bake at 400° about 20 minutes. Makes 12 muffins.

Apple-Raisin Muffins: Prepare Apple Muffins as above, *except* add ¼ cup raisins to batter.

BEST-EVER MUFFINS

The cranberry variation is shown on page 80—

- 1¾ cups all-purpose flour
- ¼ cup sugar
- 2½ teaspoons baking powder
- 1 well-beaten egg
- ¾ cup milk
- ⅓ cup cooking oil

Stir together thoroughly the first 3 ingredients and ¾ teaspoon salt; make well in center. Combine egg, milk, and oil; add all at once to dry mixture. Stir just till moistened. Fill well-greased muffin pans or paper bake cup-lined muffin pans ⅔ full. Bake at 400° for 20 to 25 minutes. Makes 12 muffins.

Blueberry-Lemon Muffins: Prepare Best-Ever Muffins as above, *except* combine ¾ to 1 cup fresh blueberries or frozen blueberries, thawed and drained, and 2 tablespoons sugar; fold into batter along with 1 teaspoon grated lemon peel. Bake as directed. While muffins are warm, dip tops in melted butter and then in sugar.

Cheese Muffins: Prepare Best-Ever Muffins as above, *except* stir ½ cup shredded sharp natural Cheddar cheese (2 ounces) into dry ingredients.

Banana-Nut Muffins: Prepare Best-Ever Muffins as above, *except* stir 1 cup chopped banana and ¼ cup chopped nuts into batter. Bake in paper bake cup-lined muffin pans for 25 to 30 minutes.

Cranberry Muffins: Prepare Best-Ever Muffins as above, *except* combine 1 cup fresh cranberries, coarsely chopped, and ¼ cup sugar; stir into batter. Bake in paper bake cup-lined pans.

Bacon Muffins: Prepare Best-Ever Muffins as above, *except* cook 4 slices bacon till crisp; drain and crumble, reserving drippings. Combine drippings with enough cooking oil to equal ⅓ cup; use in place of oil called for. Stir bacon into batter. Bake at 400° for 18 to 20 minutes.

Date-Orange-Nut Muffins: Prepare Best-Ever Muffins as above, *except* substitute ¾ cup orange juice for milk called for. *Also,* gently stir ½ cup finely chopped dates, ½ cup chopped nuts, and 1 tablespoon grated orange peel into the batter. Bake as directed.

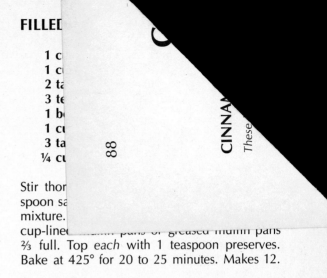

FILLED

- 1 c
- 1 c
- 2 ta
- 3 te
- 1 be
- 1 cu
- 3 ta
- ¼ cu

CINNA

These

Stir thor
spoon sa
mixture.
cup-lined muffin pans or greased muffin pans ⅔ full. Top *each* with 1 teaspoon preserves. Bake at 425° for 20 to 25 minutes. Makes 12.

BRAN-BUTTERMILK MUFFINS

- 1 cup buttermilk
- 1½ cups whole bran cereal
- ½ cup sugar
- ⅓ cup shortening
- 1 egg
- 1½ cups all-purpose flour
- 2 teaspoons baking powder
- ½ teaspoon baking soda

Add buttermilk to bran; let stand till absorbed. Cream sugar, shortening, and egg till light. Stir thoroughly the remaining ingredients and ½ teaspoon salt; blend into creamed mixture alternately with bran mixture. Stir just till combined. Fill paper bake cups ⅔ full. Bake at 400° for 20 to 22 minutes. Makes 12 muffins.

LEMONADE MUFFINS

Stir thoroughly 1¾ cups all-purpose flour, ¼ cup sugar, 2½ teaspoons baking powder, and ¾ teaspoon salt; make a well in center. Combine 1 well-beaten egg; ½ cup frozen lemonade concentrate, thawed; ¼ cup milk; and ⅓ cup cooking oil. Add all at once to dry mixture. Stir quickly just till moistened. Gently stir in ½ cup chopped walnuts. Fill greased muffin pans ⅔ full. Bake at 400° about 20 minutes. Remove from pans and brush tops with additional frozen lemonade concentrate; sprinkle generously with additional sugar. Makes 12 muffins.

Coffee Cakes and Loaves

MONJAM SQUARES

Jam-filled squares are shown on page 4 —

1½ cups all-purpose flour
½ cup granulated sugar
½ teaspoon baking powder
½ teaspoon baking soda
¼ cup butter or margarine
½ cup raisins
2 teaspoons packed brown sugar
1 teaspoon ground cinnamon
½ cup buttermilk or sour milk
1 beaten egg
¼ cup strawberry jam
Powdered sugar

Stir thoroughly the first 4 ingredients and ¼ teaspoon salt; cut in butter till mixture resembles coarse crumbs. Combine ½ *cup* of the mixture, raisins, brown sugar, and cinnamon; set aside. Beat buttermilk and egg into remaining flour mixture. Spread *half* the batter in lightly greased 8x8x2-inch baking pan; top with raisin mixture. Spoon on jam. Top with remaining batter. Bake at 350° for 35 to 40 minutes. Cool. Dust with powdered sugar.

TOASTED COCONUT COFFEE CAKE

This tasty loaf is shown on page 4 —

3 cups all-purpose flour
1 cup sugar
4 teaspoons baking powder
1 teaspoon salt
1 3½-ounce can flaked coconut, toasted
2 teaspoons shredded orange peel
1 slightly beaten egg
1½ cups milk
2 tablespoons cooking oil
1 teaspoon vanilla

Stir together thoroughly the first 4 ingredients. Stir in coconut and peel. Combine remaining ingredients; add to dry mixture all at once. Stir just till mixed. Turn batter into greased 9x5x3-inch loaf pan. Bake at 350° for 60 to 70 minutes. Remove from pan. Cool on rack. Makes 1.

RASPBERRY COFFEE CAKE

Cut one 3-ounce package cream cheese and ¼ cup butter into 2 cups packaged biscuit mix till crumbly. Blend in ⅓ cup milk. Turn out onto lightly floured surface and knead 8 to 10 strokes. On waxed paper, roll dough to 12x8-inch rectangle. Turn onto greased baking sheet; remove waxed paper. Spread ½ cup raspberry preserves down center of dough. Make 2½-inch cuts at 1-inch intervals on long sides. Fold strips over filling. Bake at 425° for 12 to 15 minutes. Drizzle the warm coffee cake with Confectioners' Icing *(see tip, page 26)*. Makes 1 coffee cake.

APPLE-NUT COFFEE CAKE

In mixing bowl cream together ½ cup shortening and 1 cup granulated sugar. Add 2 eggs and 1 teaspoon vanilla; beat well. Stir thoroughly 2 cups all-purpose flour, 1 teaspoon baking powder, 1 teaspoon baking soda, and ¼ teaspoon salt; add to creamed mixture alternately with 1 cup dairy sour cream. Fold in 2 cups finely chopped apple. Spread batter in greased 13x9x2-inch baking pan. Combine ½ cup chopped nuts, ½ cup packed brown sugar, and 1 teaspoon ground cinnamon; stir in 2 tablespoons melted butter. Sprinkle nut mixture evenly over batter. Bake at 350° for 35 to 40 minutes. Makes 1.

HONEY CRISP COFFEE CAKE

Stir to combine thoroughly 1½ cups all-purpose flour, ½ cup sugar, 2 teaspoons baking powder, ½ teaspoon salt, and ½ teaspoon mace. Drain one 8¾-ounce can crushed pineapple, reserving syrup; add enough milk to syrup to make ½ cup liquid. Combine 1 beaten egg, the pineapple liquid, and ¼ cup cooking oil; add to flour mixture, stirring till smooth. Pour into greased 9x1½-inch round baking pan. Cream ⅓ cup honey and 3 tablespoons butter till light. Add ½ cup crushed cornflakes, ¼ cup coconut, and the pineapple; mix well. Spread atop batter. Bake at 400° about 25 minutes. Makes 1.

PEANUT-HONEY COFFEE CAKE

This tasty coffee cake is shown on page 80—

> 2 cups packaged biscuit mix
> 2 tablespoons granulated sugar
> 1 slightly beaten egg
> ⅔ cup milk
> ¼ cup honey
> ¼ cup creamy peanut butter
>
> • • •
>
> ½ cup packed brown sugar
> ½ cup packaged biscuit mix
> ¼ cup chopped peanuts
> 2 tablespoons butter or margarine
> 2 tablespoons creamy peanut butter
> ½ teaspoon ground cinnamon

Stir to combine thoroughly the first 2 ingredients; add egg and milk. Blend in honey and the ¼ cup peanut butter (mixture will not be smooth). Turn into greased 9x9x2-inch baking pan. Combine remaining ingredients till crumbly; sprinkle atop batter. Bake at 400° for 20 to 25 minutes. Cool and cut into squares.

ORANGE-DATE COFFEE CAKE

> 2 cups all-purpose flour
> ½ cup granulated sugar
> 3 teaspoons baking powder
> 1 slightly beaten egg
> ½ cup milk
> ½ cup cooking oil
> ½ cup snipped dates
> 2 teaspoons grated orange peel
> ½ cup orange juice
> ½ cup chopped walnuts
> ½ cup packed brown sugar
> 2 tablespoons butter, softened
> 1 teaspoon ground cinnamon

Stir thoroughly the first 3 ingredients and ½ teaspoon salt. Combine egg, milk, and oil; add all at once to dry ingredients. Stir just till well mixed. Combine dates, peel, and juice; stir into batter just till blended. Spread evenly in greased 11x7½x1½-inch baking pan. Mix remaining ingredients; sprinkle over batter. Bake at 375° for 25 to 30 minutes. Makes 1.

Serve *Raspberry Coffee Cake* next time you need a fancy, yet quick-and-easy bread. You can make this bread with just five ingredients— biscuit mix, cream cheese, butter, milk, and raspberry preserves.

FIG BAR BREAD

1½ cups all-purpose flour
⅔ cup granulated sugar
1½ teaspoons baking powder
½ teaspoon salt
2 beaten eggs
½ cup milk
⅓ cup cooking oil
½ teaspoon vanilla
⅓ cup packed brown sugar
½ teaspoon ground cinnamon
2 tablespoons butter or margarine
6 or 7 fig bars, crumbled (1 cup)

Stir to combine thoroughly the first 4 ingredients. Combine eggs, milk, oil, and vanilla; add to flour mixture, stirring till well blended. In small bowl combine brown sugar and cinnamon; cut in butter till mixture resembles coarse crumbs. Mix in crumbled fig bars. In greased and floured 8½x4½x2½-inch loaf pan alternately layer *one-third* of batter and *half* the fig mixture, beginning and ending with batter. With narrow spatula, swirl gently through batter and crumbs to marble. Bake at 350° till done, 50 to 55 minutes. Let stand in pan 5 minutes; remove from pan. Cool on rack. Cut into thin slices; serve with butter. Makes 1 loaf.

BANANA-NUT LOAF

2 cups all-purpose flour
2 teaspoons baking powder
¾ teaspoon salt
¼ teaspoon baking soda
½ cup shortening
½ cup sugar
2 eggs
1 teaspoon grated orange peel
1 cup mashed banana
2 tablespoons milk
½ cup chopped pecans or walnuts

Stir thoroughly the first 4 ingredients. Cream shortening and sugar till light and fluffy. Add eggs and peel; beat well. Combine banana and milk; add to creamed mixture alternately with flour mixture, beating just till smooth after each addition. Stir in nuts. Turn into greased 9x5x3-inch loaf pan. Bake at 350° for 45 to 50 minutes. Wrap; store overnight. Makes 1.

PUMPKIN-NUT BREAD

This subtly spiced loaf is shown on page 80—

1 cup packed brown sugar
⅓ cup shortening
2 eggs
1 cup canned pumpkin
¼ cup milk
• • •
2 cups all-purpose flour
2 teaspoons baking powder
½ teaspoon salt
½ teaspoon ground ginger
¼ teaspoon baking soda
¼ teaspoon ground cloves
½ cup coarsely chopped walnuts

Cream together brown sugar and shortening till light and fluffy. Add eggs, one at a time, beating well after each addition. Stir in pumpkin and milk. Stir thoroughly the flour, baking powder, salt, ginger, soda, and cloves; stir into pumpkin mixture. Beat 1 minute with electric or rotary beater. Stir in nuts. Turn into greased 9x5x3-inch loaf pan. Bake at 350° for 55 to 60 minutes. Remove from pan; cool. Wrap and store overnight. Serve with butter. Makes 1.

APRICOT-BRAN BREAD

Boiling water
1 cup finely snipped dried apricots
3 tablespoons sugar
1½ cups all-purpose flour
½ cup sugar
3¾ teaspoons baking powder
1 teaspoon salt
1½ cups whole bran cereal
1 cup milk
2 beaten eggs
⅓ cup cooking oil

Pour enough boiling water over snipped apricots to cover; let stand 10 minutes. Drain well. Combine apricots and the 3 tablespoons sugar. Stir thoroughly the flour, ½ cup sugar, the baking powder, and salt. Mix bran cereal, milk, eggs, and oil; add to flour mixture, stirring just till moistened. Gently stir in apricot mixture. Turn into greased 9x5x3-inch loaf pan. Sprinkle top with a little additional sugar. Bake at 350° about 1 hour. Makes 1 loaf.

A slice of *Apricot-Bran Bread* spread generously with butter is delicious any time. And remember, this tasty bread is equally good the second day. Just wrap it in foil and store in a cool place.

NUT BREAD

3 cups all-purpose flour
1 cup sugar
4 teaspoons baking powder
1 teaspoon salt
1 beaten egg
1½ cups milk
¼ cup cooking oil
¾ cup chopped walnuts

Stir thoroughly the first 4 ingredients. Combine egg, milk, and oil; add to dry ingredients, beating well. Stir in nuts. Turn into greased 8½x4½ x2½-inch loaf pan. Bake at 350° about 70 minutes. Remove from pan; cool on rack. Makes 1.

Cheese-Nut Bread: Prepare Nut Bread as above, *except* add ¾ cup shredded natural Cheddar cheese (3 ounces) to batter with nuts.

MIDGET DATE LOAVES

1 cup boiling water
1 8-ounce package pitted dates, cut up (1¼ cups)
¼ cup shortening
1¾ cups all-purpose flour
½ cup sugar
1 teaspoon baking soda
1 beaten egg
¾ cup chopped walnuts

Pour boiling water over dates; add shortening and let stand 5 minutes. Stir to combine the flour, sugar, soda, and ¼ teaspoon salt; stir in date mixture, egg, and walnuts. Mix well. Spread batter evenly in three greased 6x3x2-inch loaf pans *or* one 9x5x3-inch loaf pan. Bake at 350° about 35 minutes for small loaves *or* 55 to 60 minutes for large loaf. Remove from pans.

SPICY CAKE DOUGHNUTS

An extra-special treat with coffee or milk—

3¼ cups all-purpose flour
2 teaspoons baking powder
½ teaspoon ground cinnamon
¼ teaspoon ground nutmeg
   Dash salt
2 eggs
⅔ cup sugar
1 teaspoon vanilla
• • •
⅔ cup light cream
¼ cup butter or margarine, melted
½ cup sugar
½ teaspoon ground cinnamon

Stir to combine thoroughly the flour, baking powder, ½ teaspoon cinnamon, nutmeg, and salt. Beat together eggs, ⅔ cup sugar, and vanilla till thick and lemon-colored. Combine light cream and melted butter or margarine. Alternately add dry ingredients and cream mixture, *half* at a time, to egg mixture. Beat just till blended after each addition. Chill dough 2 hours.

Roll dough ⅜ inch thick on floured surface; cut with floured doughnut cutter. Fry in deep hot fat (375°), turning once. (Allow about 1 minute per side.) Drain on paper toweling. Shake warm doughnuts in a mixture of the ½ cup sugar and ½ teaspoon cinnamon. Makes 20.

POPOVERS

2 eggs
1 cup milk
1 cup all-purpose flour
½ teaspoon salt
1 tablespoon cooking oil

Place eggs in mixing bowl; add milk, flour, and salt. Beat 1½ minutes with electric or rotary beater. Add cooking oil; beat mixture 30 seconds more. (Don't overbeat). Fill 6 to 8 *well-greased* custard cups ½ full. Bake at 475° for 15 minutes. Reduce heat to 350° and bake till browned and firm, 25 to 30 minutes longer. A few minutes before removing from oven, prick popovers with a fork to let steam escape.

If you like popovers dry and crisp, turn off oven and leave popovers in oven 30 minutes with door ajar. Serve hot. Makes 6 to 8 popovers.

CORN BREAD

This bread is also delicious topped with your favorite creamed meat or seafood mixture—

1 cup all-purpose flour
1 cup yellow cornmeal
¼ cup sugar
4 teaspoons baking powder
¾ teaspoon salt
2 eggs
1 cup milk
¼ cup cooking oil

Stir to combine thoroughly the first 5 ingredients. Add eggs, milk, and oil. Beat with electric or rotary beater just till smooth, about 1 minute. (Don't overbeat.) Bake in greased 9x9x2-inch baking pan at 425° for 20 to 25 minutes. Makes 8 to 9 servings.

GOLDEN CORN STICKS

Be sure to serve these warm—

¾ cup all-purpose flour
¾ cup yellow cornmeal
1 tablespoon sugar
1 teaspoon baking powder
½ teaspoon baking soda
½ teaspoon salt
1 beaten egg
1 cup dairy sour cream
2 tablespoons cooking oil

Stir thoroughly the flour, cornmeal, sugar, baking powder, soda, and salt. Combine egg, sour cream, and oil. Add to dry ingredients; stir just till blended. Preheat corn-stick pans; grease generously. Fill pans ⅔ full. Bake at 400° for 15 to 20 minutes. Makes 10 to 12.

WHEAT GERM CORN BREAD

In mixing bowl stir to combine thoroughly 1 cup all-purpose flour, ⅓ cup sugar, 5 teaspoons baking powder, and 1 teaspoon salt. Stir in 1 cup cornmeal and ¾ cup wheat germ. Combine 2 well-beaten eggs, 1½ cups milk, and ⅓ cup cooking oil. Add to flour mixture all at once; stir just to moisten. Turn into greased 9x9x2-inch baking pan. Bake at 425° for 25 to 30 minutes. Makes 9 servings.

INDEX